THE GREAT PATRIOTIC WAR
OF THE SOVIET UNION

THE GREAT PATRIOTIC WAR OF THE SOVIET UNION

BY JOSEPH STALIN

Chairman, Council of People's Commissars
Chairman, State Committee of Defense

INTERNATIONAL PUBLISHERS
NEW YORK

EDITOR'S NOTE

This collection includes the most important speeches and Orders of the Day of Marshal Stalin from the time the German rulers launched their "perfidious military attack" on the Soviet Union on June 22, 1941 until victory over Nazi Germany was achieved by the armies of the Allied coalition.

On July 3, 1941, Stalin made the historic "scorched earth" radio address to the Soviet peoples and the Red Army, mobilizing them for the patriotic war upon the fascist invaders. Following established practice, Stalin spoke next at a meeting on November 6, 1941, the eve of the twenty-fourth anniversary of the October Revolution. The following day, during a military parade on the Red Square, Stalin spoke from the reviewing stand, although the fascist hordes were outside the gates of the Soviet capital.

During the following war years, Stalin delivered reports at anniversary celebration meetings each November 6, while on November 7 he issued Orders of the Day. Similarly, on each anniversary of the founding of the Red Army, February 23, and on the occasion of May Day—a holiday in the Soviet Union—Orders of the Day were issued by Stalin, addressed not only to the fighting forces but to all the Soviet peoples who were completely mobilized behind the lines.

In each of the speeches and Orders of the Day gathered chronologically in this volume, Stalin, as head of the Soviet government and Supreme Commander-in-Chief of all the armed forces, outlined the aims and policies of the Soviet

Union and reported on the progress of its war of national liberation.

Some important policy questions are also answered by Stalin in his replies to the inquiries of representatives of the Associated Press, the *New York Times,* and Reuter agencies, and are included at the end of the book.

May 9, 1945

CONTENTS

7

8

THE GERMAN INVASION OF

THE SOVIET UNION

COMRADES! Citizens! Brothers and sisters! Men of our army and navy! I am addressing you, my friends!

The perfidious military attack on our fatherland, begun on June 22 by Hitler Germany, is continuing.

In spite of the heroic resistance of the Red Army, and although the enemy's finest divisions and finest air force units have already been smashed and have met their doom on the field of battle, the enemy continues to push forward, hurling fresh forces into the attack.

Hitler's troops have succeeded in capturing Lithuania, a considerable part of Latvia, the western part of Byelorussia, part of Western Ukraine. The fascist air force is extending the range of operations of its bombers, and is bombing Murmansk, Orsha, Mogilev, Smolensk, Kiev, Odessa, and Sebastopol.

A grave danger hangs over our country.

How could it have happened that our glorious Red Army surrendered a number of our cities and districts to fascist armies? Is it really true that German fascist troops are invincible, as is ceaselessly trumpeted by the boastful fascist propagandists?

Of course not!

History shows that there are no invincible armies and never have been. Napoleon's army was considered invincible but it was beaten successively by Russian, English, and German armies. Kaiser Wilhelm's German army in the period of the first imperialist war was also considered invincible but it was beaten several times by the Russian and Anglo-French forces and was finally smashed by the Anglo-French forces.

The same must be said of Hitler's German fascist army today. This army had not yet met with serious resistance on the continent of Europe. Only on our territory has it met serious resistance. And if, as a result of this resistance, the finest divisions of Hitler's German fascist army have been defeated by our Red Army, it means that this army too can be smashed and will be smashed as were the armies of Napoleon and Wilhelm.

As to part of our territory having nevertheless been seized by German fascist troops, this is chiefly due to the fact that the war of fascist Germany on the U.S.S.R. began under conditions favorable for the German forces and unfavorable for Soviet forces. The fact of the matter is that the troops of Germany, as a country at war, were already fully mobilized, and the one hundred and seventy divisions hurled by Germany against the U.S.S.R. and brought up to the Soviet frontiers were in a state of complete readiness, only awaiting the signal to move into action, whereas Soviet troops had still to effect mobilization and move up to the frontier.

Of no little importance in this respect is that fact that fascist Germany suddenly and treacherously violated the Non-Aggression Pact she had concluded in 1939 with the U.S.S.R., disregarding the fact that she would be regarded as the aggressor by the whole world.

Naturally, our peace-loving country, not wishing to take the initiative of breaking the pact, could not resort to perfidy.

It may be asked how could the Soviet government have consented to conclude a non-aggression pact with such treacherous fiends as Hitler and Ribbentrop? Was this not an error on the part of the Soviet government? Of course not. Non-aggression pacts are pacts of peace between states. It was such a pact that Germany proposed to us in 1939.

Could the Soviet government have declined such a proposal? I think that not a single peace-loving state could decline a peace treaty with a neighboring state, even though the latter was headed by such fiends and cannibals as Hitler and Ribbentrop. Of course only on one indispensable condition, namely, that this peace treaty does not infringe either directly or indirectly on the territorial integrity, independence, and honor of the peace-loving state. As is well known, the Non-Aggression Pact between Germany and the U.S.S.R. was precisely such a pact.

What did we gain by concluding the Non-Aggression Pact with Germany? We secured our country peace for a year and a half, and the opportunity of preparing its forces to repulse fascist Germany should she risk an attack on our country despite the pact. This was a definite advantage for us and a disadvantage for fascist Germany.

What has fascist Germany gained and what has she lost by treacherously tearing up the pact and attacking the U.S.S.R.?

She has gained a certain advantageous position for her troops for a short period, but she has lost politically by exposing herself in the eyes of the entire world as a blood-thirsty aggressor.

There can be no doubt that this short-lived military gain for Germany is only an episode, while the tremendous political gain of the U.S.S.R. is a serious and lasting factor that is bound to form the basis for the development of decisive military successes of the Red Army in the war with fascist Germany.

That is why our whole valiant Red Army, our whole valiant Navy, all our falcons of the air, all the peoples of our country, all the finest men and women of Europe, America and Asia, finally, all the finest men and women of Germany—condemn the treacherous acts of the German fascists and sympathize with the Soviet government, approve the conduct of the Soviet government, and see that ours is a just cause, that the enemy will be defeated, that we are bound to win.

By virtue of this war which has been forced upon us, our country has come to death-grips with its most malicious and most perfidious enemy—German fascism.

Our troops are fighting heroically against an enemy armed to the teeth with tanks and aircraft. Overcoming innumerable difficulties, the Red Army and Red Navy are self-sacrificingly disputing every inch of Soviet soil. The main forces of the Red Army are coming into action armed with thousands of tanks and airplanes. The men of the Red Army are displaying unexampled valor. Our resistance to the enemy is growing in strength and power.

Side by side with the Red Army, the entire Soviet people are rising in defense of our native land.

What is required to put an end to the danger hovering over our country, and what measures must be taken to smash the enemy?

Above all, it is essential that our people, the Soviet people, should understand the full immensity of the danger that threatens our country and should abandon all complacency, all heedlessness, all those moods of peaceful constructive work which were so natural before the war, but which are fatal today when war has fundamentally changed everything.

The enemy is cruel and implacable. He is out to seize our lands, watered with our sweat, to seize our grain and oil secured by our labor. He is out to restore the rule of landlords, to restore tsarism, to destroy national culture and the national state existence of the Russians, Ukrainians, Byelorussians, Lithuanians, Letts, Estonians, Uzbeks, Tatars, Moldavians, Georgians, Armenians, Azerbaidjanians, and the other free peoples of the Soviet Union, to Germanize them, to convert them into the slaves of German princes and barons.

Thus the issue is one of life or death for the Soviet State, for the peoples of the U.S.S.R.; the issue is whether the peoples of the Soviet Union shall remain free or fall into slavery.

The Soviet people must realize this and abandon all heedlessness, they must mobilize themselves and reorganize all their work on new, wartime bases, when there can be no mercy to the enemy.

Further, there must be no room in our ranks for whimperers and cowards, for panic-mongers and deserters. Our people must know no fear in fight and must selflessly join our patriotic war of liberation, our war against the fascist enslavers.

Lenin, the great founder of our state, used to say that the chief virtue of the Bolshevik must be courage, valor, fearlessness in struggle, readiness to fight, together with the people, against the enemies of our country.

This splendid virtue of the Bolshevik must become the virtue of the millions of the Red Army, of the Red Navy, of all peoples of the Soviet Union.

All our work must be immediately reconstructed on a war

13

footing, everything must be subordinated to the interests of the front and the task of organizing the demolition of the enemy.

The peoples of the Soviet Union now see that there is no taming of German fascism in its savage fury and hatred of our country, which has ensured all working people labor in freedom and prosperity.

The peoples of the Soviet Union must rise against the enemy and defend their rights and their land. The Red Army, Red Navy, and all citizens of the Soviet Union must defend every inch of Soviet soil, must fight to the last drop of blood for our towns and villages, must display the daring initiative and intelligence that are inherent in our people.

We must organize all-round assistance for the Red Army, ensure powerful reinforcements for its ranks and the supply of everything it requires, we must organize the rapid transport of troops and military freight and extensive aid to the wounded.

We must strengthen the Red Army's rear, subordinating all our work to this cause. All our industries must be got to work with greater intensity to produce more rifles, machine-guns, artillery, bullets, shells, airplanes. We must organize the guarding of factories, power-stations, telephonic and telegraphic communications, and arrange effective air raid precautions in all localities.

We must wage a ruthless fight against all disorganizers of the rear, deserters, panic-mongers, rumor-mongers, we must exterminate spies, diversionists, and enemy parachutists, rendering rapid aid in all this to our destroyer battalions.

We must bear in mind that the enemy is crafty, unscrupulous, experienced in deception and the dissemination of false rumors. We must reckon with all this and not fall victim to provocation.

All who by their panic-mongering and cowardice hinder the work of defense, no matter who they are, must be immediately haled before the military tribunal. In case of forced retreat of Red Army units, all rolling stock must be evacuated, the enemy must not be left a single engine, a single railway car, not a single pound of grain, or a gallon of fuel.

The collective farmers must drive off all their cattle, and turn over their grain to the safe-keeping of state authorities for transportation to the rear. All valuable property, including non-ferrous metals, grain, and fuel which cannot be withdrawn, must be destroyed without fail.

In areas occupied by the enemy, guerrilla units, mounted and on foot, must be formed, diversionist groups must be organized to combat the enemy troops, to foment guerrilla warfare everywhere, to blow up bridges and roads, damage telephone and telegraph lines, set fire to forests, stores, transports. In the occupied regions conditions must be made unbearable for the enemy and all his accomplices. They must be hounded and annihilated at every step, and all their measures frustrated.

This war with fascist Germany cannot be considered an ordinary war. It is not only a war between two armies, it is also a great war of the entire Soviet people against the German fascist forces.

The aim of this national war in defense of our country against the fascist oppressors is not only elimination of the danger hanging over our country, but also aid to all European peoples groaning under the yoke of German fascism.

In this war of liberation we shall not be alone. In this great

15

war we shall have loyal allies in the peoples of Europe and America, including the German people who are enslaved by the Hitlerite despots.

Our war for the freedom of our country will merge with the struggle of the peoples of Europe and America for their independence, for democratic liberties.

It will be a united front of peoples standing for freedom and against enslavement and threats of enslavement by Hitler's fascist armies.

In this connection the historic utterance of the British Prime Minister Churchill regarding aid to the Soviet Union and the declaration of the United States government signifying its readiness to render aid to our country, which can only evoke a feeling of gratitude in the hearts of the peoples of the Soviet Union, are fully comprehensible and symptomatic.

Comrades, our forces are numberless. The overweening enemy will soon learn this to his cost. Side by side with the Red Army many thousands of workers, collective farmers, intellectuals are rising to fight the enemy aggressor. The masses of our people will rise up in their millions.

The working people of Moscow and Leningrad have already commenced to form vast popular levies in support of the Red Army. Such popular levies must be raised in every city which is in danger of enemy invasion, all working people must be roused to defend our freedom, our honor, our country—in our patriotic war against German fascism.

In order to ensure the rapid mobilization of all forces of the peoples of the U.S.S.R. and to repulse the enemy who treacherously attacked our country, a State Committee of Defense has been formed in whose hands the entire power of the state has been vested.

The State Committee of Defense has entered upon its func-
tions and calls upon all our people to rally around the party
of Lenin-Stalin and around the Soviet government, so as self-
denyingly to support the Red Army and Navy, demolish the
enemy, and secure victory.

*All our forces for support of our heroic Red Army and our
glorious Red Navy!*

All forces of the people—for the demolition of the enemy!

Forward, to our victory!

Radio Address, Moscow, July 3, 1941

17

THE TWENTY-FOURTH ANNIVERSARY

OF THE OCTOBER REVOLUTION

TWENTY-FOUR YEARS have elapsed since the October Socialist Revolution triumphed and the Soviet system was established in our country. We are now standing on the threshold of the twenty-fifth year of existence of the Soviet system.

Usually at the festive sessions of the anniversary of the October Revolution the results of our successes in the field of peaceful construction for the past year are summed up. We really have the possibility of summing up such results, since our achievements in the field of peaceful construction are growing not only from year to year, but from month to month.

Both friends as well as enemies are aware of what kind of achievements these are and their extent. The past year was not a year of peaceful construction alone. It was at the same time a year of war against the German invaders, who perfidiously attacked our peace-loving country. It was only during the first six months of the past year that we were able to continue our peaceful construction. The second half of the year, over four months, is proceeding in conditions of fierce war against the German imperialists.

The war has thus become the turning point in the development of our country for the past year. The war has considerably curtailed and in some cases completely stopped our peaceful construction. It compels our whole work to be reorganized on a war footing. It has transformed our country into a single, all-embracing rear serving the front, serving our Red Army, our Red Navy.

The period of peaceful construction has ended. The period of the war of liberation against the German invaders has begun.

It is quite in place, therefore, to raise the question of the results of the war for the second half of the year, or, to be precise, for more than four months of the second half of the year, and the task we are setting ourselves in this liberation war.

I already stated in one of my speeches at the beginning of the war that the war had created a serious danger for our country, that a serious danger was facing our country, that it was necessary to understand and realize this danger and reorganize our whole work on a war footing.

Today, as a result of four months of war, I must emphasize that this danger—far from diminishing—has on the contrary increased. The enemy has captured the greater part of the Ukraine, Byelorussia, Moldavia, and Estonia, and a number of other regions, has penetrated the Donbas, is looming like a black cloud over Leningrad, and is menacing our glorious capital, Moscow.

The German fascist invaders are plundering our country, destroying the cities and villages built by the labor of the workers, peasants, and intelligentsia. The Hitler hordes are killing and violating the peaceful inhabitants of our country without sparing women, children or the aged.

Our brothers in the regions of our country captured by the Germans are groaning under the yoke of the German oppressors.

Defending the honor and freedom of the country, courageously repelling the attacks of the brutal enemy, setting examples of valor and heroism, the fighters of our army and navy have compelled the enemy to shed streams of blood.

But the enemy does not stop before sacrifices; he has not even an iota of regard for the blood of his soldiers. He is hurling ever new detachments on to the front to replace the disabled troops and is straining all his strength to capture Leningrad and Moscow before the winter sets in, for he knows that the winter holds nothing good in store for him.

In four months of the war we lost 350,000 killed, 378,000 missing, and have 1,020,000 wounded men. In the same period the enemy lost over 4,500,000 killed, wounded and prisoners. There can be no doubt that as a result of four months of the war, Germany, whose manpower reserves are already becoming exhausted, has been considerably more weakened by the war than the Soviet Union, whose reserves are only now unfolding to their full extent.

Launching their attack on our country, the German fascist invaders expected that they would surely be able to "finish" with the Soviet Union in one and a half to two months and would be able to reach the Urals within a short time.

It must be stated that the Germans did not conceal this plan for a "lightning" victory. On the contrary, they advertised it in every way. Facts, however, show how lightminded and groundless the "Blitzkrieg" plan was. It must now be considered that this mad plan has utterly failed.

How can it be explained that the "Blitzkrieg" which succeeded in Western Europe did not succeed but collapsed in the east? On what were the German fascist strategists calculating when they asserted that within two months they would finish with the Soviet Union and within this brief period reach the Urals?

They calculated primarily on the fact that they seriously hoped to create a universal coalition against the U.S.S.R., to draw Great Britain and the United States into this coalition and, preliminary to that, to frighten the ruling circles of these countries by the specter of revolution, and in this way completely isolate our country from the other powers.

The Germans knew that their policy of playing up the contradictions between classes in separate states and between these states and the Soviet country had already yielded results in France whose rulers, permitting themselves to be intimidated by the specter of revolution, in their fear placed their country at Hitler's feet and gave up resistance.

The German fascist strategists thought that the same would happen in the case of Great Britain and the United States. The not-unknown Hess was actually sent to England by the German fascists to convince the British politicians to join the universal campaign against the U.S.S.R.

But the Germans gravely miscalculated. In spite of Hess's efforts, Great Britain and the United States not only have not joined the campaign of the German fascist invaders against the U.S.S.R.; on the contrary, they are in one camp with the U.S.S.R. against Hitler Germany. The U.S.S.R. proved not only that it was not isolated; on the contrary, it acquired new allies in Great Britain, the United States and other countries occupied by the Germans.

It turned out that the German policy of playing up contradictions and intimidating by the specter of revolution has exhausted itself and no longer fits in the new situation; and not only does not fit, but is moreover pregnant with great dangers for the German invaders, for in the new conditions of war it leads to exactly the opposite result.

The Germans calculated, in the second place, on the instability of the Soviet system, the instability of the Soviet rear, in the belief that the very first serious blow and the first setbacks of the Red Army would give rise to conflicts between workers and peasants, to feuds between the peoples of the U.S.S.R., that this would be followed by uprisings and that the country would fall apart, which would make easier the advance of the German invaders as far as the Urals.

But here, too, the Germans gravely miscalculated. Far from weakening, the setbacks of the Red Army, on the contrary, strengthened still more the alliance of the workers and peasants as well as the friendship of the peoples of the U.S.S.R.

More than that, they transformed the family of the peoples of the U.S.S.R. into a single, inviolable camp which selflessly is supporting its Red Army and Red Navy.

The Soviet rear was never as strong as today. It is quite credible that with such losses as we have today, any other state would fail to withstand the ordeals and would deteriorate. If the Soviet system was able so easily to withstand the ordeal and still further to strengthen its rear, this means that the Soviet system is now the strongest system.

Finally, the German invaders calculated on the weakness of the Red Army and Red Navy, believing that with the very first blow of the German army and German navy they would scatter our army and navy and open the road for themselves for an unhampered advance into the interior of our country. But here, too, the Germans gravely miscalculated, overestimating their own forces and underestimating our army and our navy.

Of course, our army and our navy are still young; they have been fighting a mere four months; they have not yet had time to become professional in the full sense, while they are faced by the professional navy and professional army of the Germans, which have already been waging war for two years.

But, first, the morale of our army is higher than that of the German, for our army is defending its country against foreign invaders and believes in the justice of its cause, whereas the German army is waging a war of conquest and is plundering a foreign country without the possibility even for one minute of believing in the justice of their base cause.

There can be no doubt that the idea of defense of one's country, for the sake of which our people are fighting, must produce and is actually producing in our army heroes who are cementing the Red Army, whereas the idea of seizure and plunder of a foreign country, for the sake of which the Germans are actually waging war, must give rise and actually is giving rise in the German army to professional robbers devoid of any moral principles, and to the deterioration of the German army.

Secondly, advancing inland into our country, the German army is getting far away from the German rear, is compelled to act in hostile surroundings, is compelled to create a new rear in a foreign country, a rear which, moreover, is being undermined by our partisans, who are utterly disorganizing the supplies to the German army. This compels it to fear its own rear and kills its faith in the firmness of its position, at a time when our army, operating in its native surroundings, enjoys the uninterrupted support of its rear, is ensured of its supply of manpower, munitions, and foodstuffs and is firmly confident in its rear.

That is why our army has turned out to be stronger than the Germans expected, and the German army weaker than could have been supposed, judging from the boastful publicity of the German invaders.

The defense of Leningrad and Moscow, where our divisions recently annihilated some three dozen professional German divisions, shows that the new Soviet men—commanders, pilots, artillerymen, minethrowers, tankmen, infantrymen and marines—are being and already have been forged in the fire of the patriotic war and tomorrow will be the terror of the German army.

No doubt all these circumstances taken together predetermined the inevitability of the collapse of the "Blitzkrieg" in the east.

All this, of course, is true, but it is also true that along with these favorable conditions the Red Army has also to contend with a number of unfavorable conditions, through whose weight our army, suffering temporary setbacks, has been compelled to retreat, compelled to yield a number of regions of our country to the enemy.

What are these unfavorable conditions? Wherein lie the reasons for the temporary military setbacks of the Red Army?

One of the reasons for the setbacks of the Red Army consists in the absence of a second front in Europe against the German fascist troops. It is a fact that there are no armies of Great Britain or the United States on the European continent at present which are waging war against the German fascist troops, in view of which the Germans do not have to divide their forces and fight on two fronts in the west and east. And this fact brings about a situation where the Germans, considering their rear in the west secure, have the possibility of marching their troops and the armies of their allies in Europe against our country.

The situation now is such that our country is waging the war of liberation alone without anyone's military aid, against the combined forces of the Germans, Finns, Rumanians, Italians, and Hungarians.

The Germans are bragging about their temporary successes, lavishing endless praises on their army, asserting that it is able to overcome the Red Army in battles all alone. But the German assertions are empty boasting, for is it not clear why, in such a case, the Germans have resorted to the aid of the Finns, Rumanians, and Italians against the Red Army, which is fighting exclusively with its own forces without military aid from anyone?

There is no doubt that the absence of a second front against the Germans in Europe renders the position of the German army considerably easier.

But neither can there be any doubt that the appearance of a second front on the continent of Europe—and it must appear in the nearest future—will render substantially easier the position of the Red Army to the detriment of the German army.

Another reason for the temporary setbacks of our army consists in the shortage of tanks and partly also of aircraft. In modern warfare it is very difficult for the infantry to fight without tanks and without adequate protection from the air. With regard to quality, our air force is superior to the German and our glorious pilots have covered themselves with the fame of dauntless fighters, but we still have fewer planes than the Germans. The quality of our tanks is superior to that of the German tanks and our glorious tankmen and artillery men have time and again put to flight the lauded German troops with their numerous tanks. Nevertheless, we have several times fewer tanks than the Germans. Herein lies the secret of the temporary successes of the German army.

One cannot say that our tank industry is working badly or is poorly supplying our front with tanks. No, it is working very well and producing no small number of splendid tanks. But the Germans are producing a far greater number of tanks because they now have at their disposal not only their own tank industry but also the industries of Czechoslovakia, Belgium, Holland, and France. Were it not for this fact, the Red Army would long ago have smashed the German army, which never goes into battle without tanks and cannot withstand the blows of our units unless it has superiority in tanks.

There is only one means necessary to reduce the German superiority in tanks to naught and thereby radically to change the position of both armies. This consists not only in achieving a several-fold increase in the tank production in our country, but also in achieving a sharp increase in production of anti-tank rifles and guns, anti-tank grenades and mine-throwers, in building more anti-tank pits and all sorts of other anti-tank obstacles. This constitutes the task at present. We can fulfill this task and we must fulfill it at any cost.

In our country the German invaders, that is the Hitlerites, are usually referred to as fascists. The Hitlerites, it turns out, consider this incorrect and persist in calling themselves "National-Socialists." Consequently, the Germans want to convince us that the party of the Hitlerites, the party of the German invaders, which is robbing Europe and which has organized the villainous attack on our socialist state, is a socialist party. Is this possible? Can there be anything in common between socialism and the brutal Hitlerite invaders who are robbing and oppressing the peoples of Europe? Can the Hitlerites be considered nationalists? Actually, the Hitlerites today are not nationalists but imperialists. While the Hitlerites were uniting German lands and incorporating the Rhine region, Austria, and others, they could in a certain sense be considered nationalists. But after they captured foreign territories and enslaved European nations—the Czechs, Slovaks, Poles, Norwegians, Danes, Dutch, Belgians, Frenchmen, Serbs, Greeks, Ukrainians, Byelorussians, and the Baltic peoples, and so forth,—and began to drive for world domination, the Hitler party ceased to be nationalist, for from that moment it became a party of imperialism, conquest, and oppression.

The party of the Hitlerites is a party of imperialists, moreover, the most rapacious and plunderous imperialists among all the imperialists of the world. Can the Hitlerites be considered Socialists? No, they cannot. In fact, the Hitlerites are the avowed enemies of socialism, the bitterest reactionaries and blackguards who have deprived the working class and peoples of Europe of their elementary democratic liberties. To cover up their reactionary, blackguard essence, the Hitlerites are branding the Anglo-American internal regime as a plutocratic regime. But in England and the United States there are elementary democratic liberties, there are trade unions of workers and employees, there are labor parties, there is a parliament, whereas the Hitler regime has abolished all these institutions in Germany.

It is sufficient to compare these two series of facts to understand the reactionary essence of the Hitler regime and the full falseness of the chatter of the German fascists about the Anglo-American plutocratic regime.

Actually the Hitler regime is a counterpart of the reactionary regime which existed in Russia under tsarism. It is known that the Hitlerites today as readily violate the rights of the workers, the rights of the intelligentsia, the rights of the peoples, as these were violated by the tsarist regime; that they today as readily organize medieval Jewish pogroms as they were organized by the tsarist regime.

The Hitler party is a party of the enemies of democratic liberties, a party of medieval reaction and blackguard pogroms. And if these brazen imperialists and most bitter reactionaries still continue to parade in the cloak of "nationalists" and "Socialists," they are doing it in order to deceive the people, befuddle simpletons and cover their robber imperialism in essence with the flag of "nationalism" and "socialism." The crow is donning peacock feathers—but, however much crows adorn themselves with peacock feathers, they cannot cease to be crows.

"We must strive by any means," Hitler said, "to have the world conquered by Germans. If we want to create our great German empire, we must above all force out and exterminate the Slav peoples, the Russians, Poles, Czechs, Slovaks, Bulgarians, Ukrainians and Byelorussians. There are no reasons to prevent us from doing this."

"Man," says Hitler, "is sinful from the moment of his birth and can be ruled only by force. Any methods are permissible in treating him. When politics require it, it is necessary to lie, betray and even kill."

"Kill everyone who is against us," Goering says. "Kill and kill again; I and not you bear responsibility for it, therefore kill!"

"I am freeing man from the degrading chimera called conscience," says Hitler. "Conscience, like education, cripples man.

28

I have the advantage of not being deterred by any considerations of theoretical or moral order."

One of the orders of the German command to the 459th Regiment, dated September 25 and found on a dead German, reads as follows: "I order firing at every Russian as soon as he appears within six hundred meters distance. The Russian must know that he is faced with a resolute enemy from whom he cannot expect any lenience."

One of the appeals of the German command to the soldiers, found on dead Lieutenant Gustav Ziegal, a native of Frankfurt-on-Main, reads: "You have neither heart nor nerves; they are not needed in war. Free yourselves from feelings of compassion and sympathy—kill every Russian, every Soviet person. Don't stop, whether you have an old man, a woman, a girl or a boy before you—kill. Thereby you will save yourselves from death, secure the future of your family and win eternal glory."

There you have the program and directives of the leaders of the Hitlerite party and Hitlerite command, the program and directives of people who have lost every vestige of human beings and are degraded to the level of wild beasts. And these people, deprived of conscience and honor, people with the morals of beasts, have the audacity to call for the annihilation of the great Russian nation, the nation of Plekhanov and Lenin, Belinsky and Chernyshevsky, Pushkin and Tolstoy, Glinka and Tschaikowsky, Gorky and Chekhov, Sechenov and Pavlov, Repin and Surikov, Suvorov and Kutuzov!

The German invaders want a war of extermination against the peoples of the U.S.S.R. Well, if the Germans want a war of extermination, they shall have it.

Henceforth our task, the task of the peoples of the U.S.S.R., the task of the men, commanders and political workers of our army and our navy, consists in annihilating to the last man all Germans who penetrated the territory of our country as its occupationists.

No mercy to the German occupationists! Death to the German occupationists!

The rout of the German imperialists and their armies is inevitable. The fact alone that in their moral degradation the German invaders, having lost the human aspect, have already sunk to the level of wild beasts—this fact alone shows that they have doomed themselves to inevitable death.

But the inevitable death of the Hitler invaders and their armies is determined not by moral factors alone.

There are three other basic factors whose force is growing from day to day and which must in the near future lead to the inevitable rout of the Hitler robber imperialists. These are, first, the instability of the European rear of imperialist Germany, the instability of the "new order" in Europe. The German invaders have enslaved the peoples of the European continent from France to the Soviet Baltic, from Norway, Denmark, Belgium, Holland, and Soviet Byelorussia to the Balkans and the Soviet Ukraine, have deprived them of their elementary democratic liberties, deprived them of the right to control their own destiny, deprived them of grain, meat, and raw materials, converted them into their slaves, crucified the Poles, Czechs, and Serbs, and decided that by achieving the domination of Europe they would be able to build Germany's world domination on this basis. That is what they call the "new order in Europe."

But what is this "basis," what is this "new order"? Only the Hitlerite self-adulating fools fail to see that the "new order" in Europe and the notorious "basis" of this order constitute a volcano ready to erupt at any moment and bury the German imperialist house of cards. Some refer to Napoleon, asserting that Hitler is acting like Napoleon and that he has every resemblance to Napoleon. But, first, Napoleon's fate must not be forgotten. Secondly, Hitler no more resembles Napoleon than a kitten resembles a lion, for Napoleon fought against the forces of reaction and was supported by progressive forces, and Hitler, on the contrary, is supported by reactionary forces, is waging a struggle against the progressive forces.

Only the Hitlerite fools from Berlin can fail to understand that the enslaved peoples of Europe will fight and will rise against Hitler tyranny. Who can doubt that the U.S.S.R., Great Britain and the United States will render full aid to the peoples of Europe in their liberation struggle against Hitler tyranny?

Secondly, the instability of the German rear of the Hitlerite invaders. While the Hitlerites were uniting Germany, dismembered under the Versailles Treaty, they could have the support of the German people, inspired by the idea of the restoration of Germany. But after this task was solved and the Hitlerites took to the path of imperialism, to the path of seizure of foreign lands and conquest of foreign peoples, having converted the peoples of Europe and the peoples of the U.S.S.R. into avowed enemies of present-day Germany, the German people have taken the profound turn of opposing the war and are in favor of liquidation of the war.

More than two years of bloody war, the end of which is not in sight; millions of human victims, hunger, pauperization, epidemics, the hostile atmosphere surrounding the Germans, Hitler's stupid policy which transformed the peoples of the U.S.S.R. into avowed enemies of present-day Germany—all this could not but turn the German people against the need-less and ruinous war.

Only Hitlerite fools can fail to understand that not only the European rear but also the German rear of the German troops represent a volcano ready to erupt and bury the Hitler adventurists.

And finally there is the coalition of the U.S.S.R., Great Britain, and the United States against the German fascist imperialists. It is a fact that Great Britain, the United States, and the Soviet Union have united into a single camp which has set itself the task of crushing the Hitler imperialists and their armies of conquest. The present war is a war of motors. He who will have the overwhelming superiority in the production of motors will win the war. If we combine the output of the motors of the United States, Great Britain, and the U.S.S.R. we will have a superiority in motors of at least three to one as compared with Germany. Herein lies one of the bases of the inevitable doom of Hitler's robber imperialism.

The recent three-power conference in Moscow with the participation of the representative of Great Britain, Mr. Beaverbrook, and of the representative of the United States, Mr. Harriman, decided systematically to assist our country with tanks and aircraft. As is known, we already have begun to receive shipments of tanks and planes on the basis of this decision.

Still earlier, Great Britain ensured the supply to our country of such needed materials as aluminum, lead, tin, nickel, and rubber.

If to this is added the fact that recently the United States decided to grant a billion dollar loan to the Soviet Union, it can be confidently said that the coalition of the United States,

Great Britain, and the U.S.S.R. is a real thing which is growing and which will continue to grow for the benefit of our common cause of liberation. Such are the factors determining the inevitable death of German fascist imperialism.

Lenin distinguished between two kinds of wars: wars of conquest, and consequently unjust wars, and wars of liberation—just wars. The Germans are now waging a war of conquest—an unjust war with the object of seizure of foreign territory and the subjugation of foreign peoples. Therefore all honest people must rise up against the German invaders as against enemies. Unlike Hitler Germany, the Soviet Union and its allies are waging a war for the liberation of the enslaved peoples of Europe and the U.S.S.R. from Hitler tyranny. Therefore, all honest people must support the armies of the U.S.S.R., Great Britain, and the other allies, as armies of liberation.

We have not and cannot have such war aims as the seizure of foreign territories, the subjugation of foreign peoples, regardless of whether it concerns peoples and territories of Europe or peoples and territories of Asia, including Iran. Our first aim consists in liberating our territory and our peoples from the German fascist yoke.

We have not and cannot have such war aims as imposing our will and our regime on the Slavs and other enslaved peoples of Europe who are awaiting our aid. Our aid consists in assisting these people in their liberation struggle against Hitler tyranny and then setting them free to rule on their own land as they desire. No intervention whatever in the internal affairs of other peoples!

But to realize these aims it is necessary to crush the military might of the German invaders; it is necessary to annihilate

33

to a man all the German occupationists who penetrated our country in order to enslave it.

But for this it is necessary that our army and our navy should have the active, energetic support of our whole country, that our workers and employees, men and women, should work ceaselessly at the enterprises and should produce ever more tanks, anti-tank guns, planes, cannon, mine-throwers, machine guns, rifles and munitions for the front, that our collective farmers, men and women, should work tirelessly in their fields producing ever greater quantities of grain and meat for the front and for the country and raw materials for industry, that our whole country and all peoples of the U.S.S.R. should organize into a single war camp which together with our army and navy would wage a great liberation war for the honor and freedom of our country, for routing the German armies.

This constitutes the task at present. We can and must carry out this task. Only by carrying out this task and crushing the German invaders can we achieve a lasting, just peace.

For the complete rout of the German invaders!

For the liberation of all oppressed peoples groaning under the yoke of Hitler tyranny!

Long live the inviolable friendship of the peoples of the Soviet Union!

Long live our Red Army and Navy!

Long live our glorious country!

Our cause is just; victory will be ours!

Speech delivered at Moscow,
November 6, 1941

THE TWENTY-FOURTH ANNIVERSARY

OF THE OCTOBER REVOLUTION

COMRADES, Red Army and Red Navy men, commanders and political instructors, men and women workers, men and women collective farmers, intellectuals, brothers and sisters in the enemy rear who have temporarily fallen under the yoke of the German brigands, our glorious men and women guerrillas who are disrupting the rear of the German invaders:

On behalf of the Soviet government and our Bolshevik Party I greet you and congratulate you on the twenty-fourth anniversary of the great October Socialist Revolution.

Comrades, today we must celebrate the twenty-fourth anniversary of the October Revolution in difficult conditions. The German brigands' treacherous attack and the war that they forced upon us have created a threat to our country. We have temporarily lost a number of regions, and the enemy is before the gates of Leningrad and Moscow.

The enemy calculated that our army would be dispersed at the very first blow and our country forced to its knees. But the enemy wholly miscalculated. Despite temporary reverses, our army and our navy are bravely beating off enemy attacks along the whole front, inflicting heavy losses, while our country —our whole country—has organized itself into a single fighting camp in order, jointly with our army and navy, to rout the German invaders.

There was a time when our country was in a still more difficult position. Recall the year 1918, when we celebrated the first anniversary of the October Revolution. At that time three-quarters of our country was in the hands of foreign interventionists. We had temporarily lost the Ukraine, the Caucasus, Central Asia, the Urals, Siberia, and the Far East. We had no allies, we had no Red Army—we had only just begun to create it—and we experienced a shortage of bread, a shortage of arms, a shortage of equipment.

At that time fourteen states were arrayed against our country, but we did not become despondent or downhearted. In the midst of the conflagration of war we organized the Red Army and converted our country into a military camp. The spirit of the great Lenin inspired us at that time for the war against the interventionists.

And what happened? We defeated the interventionists, we regained all our lost territories and we achieved victory.

Today our country is in a far better position than it was twenty-three years ago. Today it is many times richer in industry, food, and raw materials. Today we have allies who jointly with us form a united front against the German invaders. Today we enjoy the sympathy and support of all the peoples of Europe fallen under the yoke of fascist tyranny. Today we have a splendid army and a splendid navy, defending the freedom and independence of our country with their lives. We experience no serious shortage either of food or of arms or equipment.

Our whole country, all the peoples of our country, are backing our army and our navy, helping them smash the Nazi hordes. Our reserves in manpower are inexhaustible. The spirit of the great Lenin inspires us in our patriotic war today as it did twenty-three years ago.

Is it possible, then, to doubt that we can and must gain victory over the German invaders? The enemy is not as strong as some terror-stricken would-be intellectuals picture him. The devil is not as terrible as he is painted. Who can deny that our Red Army has more than once put the much-lauded German troops to panicky flight?

If one judges by Germany's real position and not by the boastful assertions of German propagandists, it will not be difficult to see that the Nazi German invaders are facing disaster.

Hunger and poverty reign in Germany. In four and a half months of war Germany has lost four and a half million soldiers. Germany is bleeding white; her manpower is giving out. A spirit of revolt is gaining possession not only of the nations of Europe under the German invaders' yoke, but of the Germans themselves, who see no end to the war.

The German invaders are straining their last forces. There is no doubt that Germany cannot keep up such an effort for any long time. Another few months, another half year, one year perhaps—and Hitlerite Germany must collapse under the weight of its own crimes.

Comrades, Red Army and Red Navy men, commanders and political instructors, men and women guerrillas:

The whole world is looking to you as a force capable of destroying the brigand hordes of German invaders. The enslaved peoples of Europe under the yoke of the German invaders are looking to you as their liberators. A great mission of liberation has fallen to your lot.

Be worthy of this mission! The war you are waging is a

war of liberation, a just war. Let the manly images of our great ancestors—Alexander Nevsky, Dmitri Donskoi, Kusma Minin, Dmitri Pozharsky, Alexander Suvorov, Mikhail Kutuzov—inspire you in this war!

Let the victorious banner of the great Lenin fly over your heads!

Utter destruction to the German invaders!

Death to the German armies of occupation!

Long live our glorious motherland, her freedom and her independence!

Under the banner of Lenin—onward to victory!

Speech on Red Square, November 7, 1941

THE TWENTY-FOURTH ANNIVERSARY
OF THE FOUNDING OF THE
RED ARMY

COMRADES, Red Army and Red Navy men, commanders and political workers, guerrillas—men and women:

The peoples of our country celebrate the twenty-fourth anniversary of the Red Army in stern days of patriotic war against fascist Germany, which is insolently and basely encroaching upon the life and freedom of our motherland.

Along a tremendous front, from the Arctic Ocean to the Black Sea, Red Army and Red Navy men are fighting fierce battles to drive the German fascist invaders from our country and safeguard the honor and independence of our motherland.

It is not the first time that the Red Army has had to defend our native land from enemy attack. The Red Army was created twenty-four years ago to fight the troops of foreign interventionist invaders, who strove to dismember our country and destroy its independence.

Young detachments of the Red Army, which were taking part in a war for the first time, inflicted utter defeat on the German invaders at Pskov and Narva on February 23, 1918. For this reason the day of February 23, 1918, was proclaimed the birthday of the Red Army.

After that the Red Army grew and gained strength in the struggle against the foreign interventionist invaders. It safeguarded our native land in battles with the German invaders in 1918 and drove them from the Ukraine and Byelorussia.

It protected our native land in battles with foreign troops of the Entente from 1918 to 1921 and drove them from our country.

The defeat of the foreign interventionist invaders in the time of the Civil War secured to the peoples of the Soviet Union a lasting peace and the possibility of peaceful constructive work. A socialist industry and a collective agriculture grew up in our country. Science and culture flourished. The friendship of the peoples of our native land grew strong.

But the Soviet people never forgot the possibility that our enemies might make a fresh attack on our country. Therefore, simultaneously with the development of industry and agriculture, science and culture, the military strength of the Soviet Union grew also. Certain seekers after foreign lands have felt this strength on their own hides. The much advertised German fascist army is feeling it now.

Eight months ago fascist Germany treacherously attacked our country, crudely violating a treaty of non-aggression. The enemy expected that at the very first blow the Red Army would be routed and would lose the ability to resist. But the enemy badly miscalculated. He did not realize the power of the Red Army, did not realize the strength of the Soviet rear, did not realize the determination of our country's peoples to win, did not realize the unreliability of fascist Germany's European rear, and lastly did not realize the internal weakness of fascist Germany and its army.

In the first months of the war, as a result of the unexpectedness and suddenness of the German fascist attack, the Red Army was forced to retreat and evacuate part of our territory. But, while retreating, it wore down the enemy forces and dealt them heavy blows. Neither the Red Army men nor the peoples of our country doubted that this retreat was temporary, that the enemy would be checked and then defeated.

As the war progressed, the Red Army accumulated fresh, vital strength. It was reinforced with men and equipment. It received fresh reserve divisions to assist it. There came a time when the Red Army was able to take the offensive in the principal sectors of the tremendous front. Within a short time the Red Army dealt the German fascist troops one blow after another—at Rostov-on-Don and Tikhvin, in the Crimea and at Moscow.

In the violent battles at Moscow it defeated the German fascist troops which threatened to encircle the Soviet capital. The Red Army threw the enemy back from Moscow and continues to push him westward. The Moscow and Tula Regions have been completely freed from the German invaders, as have dozens of towns and hundreds of villages in other regions temporarily seized by the enemy.

Now the Germans no longer possess the military advantage which they had in the first months of the war by virtue of their treacherous and sudden attack. The momentum of unexpectedness and suddenness which constituted the reserve strength of the German fascist troops has been fully spent.

Thus, the inequality in the conditions under which the war was conducted, created by the suddenness of the German fascist attack, has been eliminated. Henceforward the issue of the war will not be decided by such a secondary factor as suddenness, but by such constantly operating factors as the strength of the rear, the morale of the army, the quantity and quality of the divisions, the armament of the army, the organizational abilities of the army commanders.

One circumstance should be noted in this connection: No

sooner did the German arsenal lose the weapon of suddenness than the German army was confronted with catastrophe.

The German fascists consider their army invincible, asserting that man for man it can undoubtedly defeat the Red Army. At present the Red Army and the German fascist army are fighting on equal terms, man for man. Moreover, the German fascist army is directly supported at the front by the troops of Italy, Rumania and Finland. The Red Army so far has no such support. And what happens? The much lauded German army is suffering defeat, while the Red Army is scoring important victories.

Falling back westward under the powerful blows of the Red Army, the German troops are suffering tremendous losses in manpower and equipment. They are clinging to every fold of ground to postpone the day of their utter defeat. But the enemy's efforts are in vain.

The initiative is now in our hands, and the efforts of Hitler's loose and rusty machine cannot check the Red Army's onslaught. The day is not distant when the Red Army's powerful blows will drive the enemy from Leningrad, clear him from the towns and villages of Byelorussia and the Ukraine, from Lithuania and Latvia, from Estonia and Karelia, will free Soviet Crimea, and the red banners will again fly victoriously over the whole Soviet land.

It would, however, be unpardonable nearsightedness to rest content with the success achieved and to believe that we have already finished with the German troops. This would be empty boasting and conceit unworthy of the Soviet people. It must not be forgotten that there are still many difficulties ahead.

The enemy is suffering defeat, but he has not yet been

routed, and still less finished off. The enemy is still strong. He will exert the last remnants of his strength to attain success. And the more defeats he suffers, the more furious he will become.

It is therefore necessary that the training of reserves to assist the front should not relax in our country for a single minute. It is necessary that fresh army units should go to the front one after another to forge victory over the bestial enemy. It is necessary that our industry, especially our war industry, should work with redoubled vigor. It is necessary that the front should receive daily increasing quantities of tanks, planes, guns, trench mortars, machine guns, rifles, automatic rifles, and ammunition.

This is one of the Red Army's main sources of strength and might. But it is not the Red Army's only source of strength. The Red Army's strength lies above all in the fact that it is not waging a predatory, imperialist war, but a patriotic war, a war of liberation, a just war.

The Red Army's task is to free our Soviet territory from the German invaders, to free from the yoke of the German invaders the residents of our villages and towns, who were free and lived like human beings before the war and now are oppressed and suffer pillage, ruin, and famine, and lastly to free our women from the disgrace and outrage to which they are subjected by the German fascist fiends. What could be nobler and loftier than this task?

No single German soldier can say that he is waging a just war, because he cannot fail to see that he is forced to fight in order to plunder and oppress other peoples. The German soldier lacks a lofty, noble aim in the war which could inspire him and in which he could take pride. On the contrary, the

43

Red Army man can proudly say that he is waging a just war, a war for liberation, a war for the freedom and independence of his motherland.

The Red Army pursues a noble and lofty war aim, which inspires it to heroic feats. This, properly speaking, explains why the patriotic war brings forward thousands of heroes and heroines in our country, ready to face death for the freedom of their motherland. This is a source of strength to the Red Army. This is also a source of weakness to the German fascist army.

Occasionally the foreign press engages in prattle to the effect that the Red Army's aim is to exterminate the German people and destroy the German state. This is, of course, a stupid lie and a witless slander against the Red Army. The Red Army has not and cannot have such idiotic aims. The Red Army's aim is to drive out the German occupants from our country and liberate Soviet soil from the German fascist invaders.

It is very likely that the war for liberation of the Soviet land will result in ousting or destroying Hitler's clique. We should welcome such an outcome. But it would be ridiculous to identify Hitler's clique with the German people and the German state. History shows that Hitlers come and go, but the German people and the German state remain.

Lastly, the strength of the Red Army lies in the fact that it does not and cannot entertain racial hatred for other peoples, including the German people, that it has been brought up in the spirit of the equality of all peoples and races, in the spirit of respect for the rights of other peoples.

The Germans' racial theory and their practice of racial hatred have brought about a situation in which all freedom-loving peoples have become enemies of fascist Germany. The theory of race equality in the U.S.S.R. and the practice of respect for the rights of other peoples have brought about a situation in which all freedom-loving peoples have become friends of the Soviet Union. This is a source of strength to the Red Army. This is also a source of weakness to the German fascist army.

Sometimes the foreign press engages in prattle to the effect that the Soviet people hates the Germans just because they are Germans, that the Red Army exterminates German soldiers just because they are Germans, because it hates everything German, and that therefore the Red Army does not take German soldiers prisoner. This is, of course, a similar stupid lie and witless slander against the Red Army. The Red Army is free of feelings of racial hatred. It is free of such humiliating feelings because it has been brought up in the spirit of racial equality and respect for the rights of other peoples. Besides, one should not forget that in our country any manifestation of racial hatred is punished by law.

Certainly the Red Army must annihilate the German fascist occupants, since they wish to enslave our motherland, and when, being surrounded by our troops, they refuse to lay down their arms and surrender. The Red Army annihilates them not because of their German origin but because they wish to enslave our motherland. The Red Army, like the army of any other people, is entitled and bound to annihilate the enslavers of its motherland, irrespective of their national origin.

Recently the German garrisons stationed in Kalinin, Klin, Sukhinichi, Andreapol, and Toropets were surrounded by our troops, who offered to let them surrender and promised to spare their lives. The German garrisons refused to lay down their arms and surrender. It is clear that they had to be driven out by force, and not a few Germans were killed. War is war.

The Red Army takes German soldiers and officers prisoner if they surrender, and spares their lives. The Red Army annihilates German soldiers and officers if they refuse to lay down their arms and when they attempt, arms in hand, to enslave our motherland. Recall the words of the great Russian writer Maxim Gorki: "If the enemy does not surrender, he is annihilated."

Comrades, Red Army and Red Navy men, commanders and political workers, guerrillas—men and women: I congratulate you on the twenty-fourth anniversary of the Red Army. I wish you complete victory over the German fascist invaders.

Long live the Red Army and Navy!

Long live the guerrillas, men and women!

Long live our glorious motherland, its freedom and independence!

Long live the great Party of the Bolsheviks, leading us to victory!

Long live the invincible banner of the great Lenin!

Under Lenin's banner, onward to defeat the German fascist invaders!

Order of the Day,
February 23, 1942

46

MAY DAY, 1942

Comrades, Red Army men and Red Navy men, commanders and political personnel, men and women guerrilla fighters, workingmen and working women, peasants, intellectuals, brothers and sisters behind the German fascist lines temporarily fallen under the yoke of German oppressors:

On behalf of the Soviet Government and our Bolshevik Party, I extend to you greetings and congratulations on the occasion of May Day.

Comrades, the peoples of our country observe international May Day this year in the midst of the patriotic war against the German fascist invaders. War has left its imprint on all aspects of our life. It has left its imprint on this day, May Day, too.

In view of the war situation, the working people of our country have denied themselves the holiday in order to devote this day to intensive work for our country's defense. Having one common interest with our fighters at the front, they have made May Day a day of labor and struggle in order to render the front the greatest possible aid and to provide it with more rifles, machine-guns, cannon, mortars, tanks, aircraft, munitions, bread, meat, fish, vegetables.

This signifies that our front and rear form one indissoluble fighting camp, prepared to surmount all difficulties on our path to victory over the enemy.

Comrades, over two years have elapsed since the German fascist invaders plunged Europe into the abyss of war, subjugated the freedom-loving nations of continental Europe—France, Norway, Denmark, Belgium, Holland, Czechoslovakia, Poland, Jugoslavia, Greece—and are bleeding them white, so that the German bankers may become still richer.

More than ten months have passed since the German fascist invaders foully and perfidiously attacked our country and began to loot and devastate our cities and villages, violate and kill the peaceful population of Esthonia, Latvia, Lithuania, Byelo-Russia, the Ukraine and Moldavia.

More than ten months have passed since the peoples of our country began the patriotic war against the bestial enemy in defense of the honor and liberty of their homeland. During this period we have had ample opportunity to study the German fascists, to understand their real intentions and to see them in their true colors, not merely on the basis of their statements, but on the basis of the experience of war, on the basis of generally known facts.

Who are they, our enemies, these German fascists? What sort of people are they? What does the experience of war teach us in this respect?

It is said that the German fascists are nationalists, upholding the integrity and independence of Germany against the encroachment of other nations. This, of course, is a lie. Only liars can assert that Norway, Denmark, Belgium, Holland, Greece, the Soviet Union and other freedom-loving countries encroached on Germany's territorial integrity and independence.

In actual fact the German fascists are not nationalists but imperialists who seize other countries and bleed them white

48

to enrich German bankers and plutocrats. Goering, the head of the German fascists, is himself, as we know, one of the richest bankers and plutocrats, exploiting dozens of factories and mills. Hitler, Goebbels, Ribbentrop, Himmler, and other rulers of present-day Germany are but watchdogs of the German bankers and place the latter's interests above all other interests. In their hands the German army is a blind tool, destined to shed its own blood and the blood of other peoples, to cripple itself and others, not for the sake of Germany's interests, but for the enrichment of German bankers and plutocrats.

That is what the experience of war shows.

We are told that the German fascists are socialists, seeking to defend the interests of the workers and peasants against the plutocrats.

This, of course, is a lie. Only liars can assert that the German fascists, who have introduced slave labor in the factories and mills and resurrected serfdom in the German villages and in the vanquished countries, are champions of the workers and peasants. Only brazen deceivers can deny that the slave and serf system set up by the German fascists is advantageous to the German plutocrats and bankers and not to the workers and peasants.

In actual fact, the German fascists are reactionary feudal barons and the German army is an army dominated by feudal barons and shedding its blood to enrich the German barons and re-establish the rule of landlords.

That is what the experience of war shows.

We are told that the German fascists are promoters of European culture, and that they are waging a war to extend this culture to other countries. This, of course, is a lie. Only professional deceivers can assert that the German fascists who have covered Europe with scaffolds, who are looting and violating peaceful populations, burning and blowing up towns and villages, and laying waste to the cultural treasures of the peoples of Europe, can be promoters of European culture.

In actual fact, the German fascists are enemies of European culture and the German army is an army of medieval obscurantism, employed to destroy European culture and implant the slave-owners' "culture" of the German bankers and barons.

That is what the experience of war shows.

Such is our enemy in his true colors, exposed and brought to light by the experience of war.

But the experience of war is not limited to these conclusions. The experience of war shows also that in the course of the war serious changes have taken place, both in the position of fascist Germany and her army and in the position of our country and our Red Army.

What are these changes?

First of all, during this period fascist Germany and her army are undoubtedly weaker than they were ten months ago. War has brought the German people great disillusionment, loss of millions of human lives, hunger, and poverty. The end of the war is not in sight, but Germany's man-power reserves are running low, oil and raw material stocks are also running low. The realization of Germany's inevitable defeat is constantly growing among the German people. It is becoming increasingly clear to the German people that the only way out of the present situation is the liberation of Germany from the Hitler-Goering adventurist clique.

Hitler imperialism has occupied extensive territory in Europe, but it has not broken the will of the European peoples to resist. The struggle of the subjugated nations against the regime of the German fascist marauders is beginning to assume a universal character. In all the occupied lands sabotage in war industry, explosions of German supply depots, wrecking of German troop trains, murder of German soldiers and officers have become a common occurrence. The whole of Jugoslavia and the German-occupied Soviet districts are enveloped in the flames of guerrilla war. These factors have resulted in the weakening of the German rear, and consequently in weakening fascist Germany as a whole.

As for the Germany army, despite its stubbornness in defense, it is nevertheless much weaker than ten months ago. Its old experienced generals—Reichenau, Brauchitsch, Todt and others—have been either killed by the Red Army or ousted by the German fascist leadership, its regular officer corps has been partly annihilated by the Red Army and partly disintegrated as a result of the looting and violence against the civil population. Its rank and file has been materially weakened in the course of hostilities and receives less and less reinforcement.

Secondly, during this period our country undoubtedly has become stronger than it was at the beginning of the war.

Not only our friends, but our foes as well, are constrained to admit that our country is united more than ever before and has rallied around its government; that its rear and front are united in a single fighting camp, directing its efforts to one purpose; and that the Soviet people in the rear provide our front with ever increasing quantities of rifles and machine-guns, mortars and cannon, tanks and aircraft, provisions and ammunition.

As for the international contacts of our country, these have of late become stronger and broader than ever. All freedom-loving peoples have united against German imperialism. Their eyes are turned to the Soviet Union. The heroic struggle which the peoples of our country are waging for their liberty, honor and independence evokes the admiration of all progressive mankind. The peoples of all freedom-loving countries regard the Soviet Union as the force capable of saving the world from the Hitler plague. Among these freedom-loving countries, the first place belong to Great Britain and the United States of America, with whom we are bound by ties of friendship and who render our country more and more military aid against the German fascist invaders.

All these factors testify that our country has become much stronger.

Lastly, in the past period the Red Army has undoubtedly become more organized and stronger than at the beginning of the war. It is a well known fact that following the temporary withdrawal caused by the German imperialists' perfidious attack, the Red Army turned the tide of war and went over from active defense to a successful offensive against enemy troops. This cannot be regarded as accidental. It is a fact that the successes of the Red Army have brought the patriotic war into a new phase—the phase of liberation of Soviet territory from the Hitler scum. True, the Red Army began the fulfillment of this historic task under the difficult conditions of severe winter, of heavy snows, but it nevertheless achieved major successes.

Having taken over the initiative, the Red Army inflicted several hard-felt defeats on the German troops and compelled them to clear a considerable part of Soviet territory. The invader's plans to use the winter for rest and for consolidating his defense line suffered collapse. In the course of its advance, the Red Army destroyed an enormous amount of enemy manpower and materiel, captured no small quantity of materiel and compelled the enemy prematurely to use up the reserves brought up from the deep rear and intended for the spring and summer operations. All of this shows that the Red Army has become more organized and stronger, that its officers corps have been steeled in battle and its generals have acquired greater experience and foresight.

A change has also taken place in the rank and file of the Red Army. Complacency and frivolousness with regard to the enemy, which was observed among Red Army men in the first months of the patriotic war, have disappeared. The atrocities, pillage, and violence perpetrated by the German fascist invaders against the peaceful population and Soviet war prisoners have cured our men of this disease. Red Army men have become more bitter and ruthless. They have learned really to hate the German fascist invaders. They realize that one cannot defeat the enemy without learning to hate him with every fiber of one's soul. Gone is the prattle about the invincibility of German troops which was observed at the beginning of the war and which concealed a fear of the Germans. The renowned battles at Rostov and Kerch, Moscow and Kalinin, Tikhvin and Leningrad, where the Red Army put the German fascist invaders to flight, convinced our men that this prattle about German invincibility is simply a fairy tale concocted by the fascist propagandists.

The experience of war has convinced our Red Army man that the so-called bravery of the German officer is a very relative thing, that the German officer is brave against unarmed war prisoners or peaceful civilians, but that he loses all bravery as soon as he is faced with the Red Army's organized might. Remember the popular Russian saying: "Brave against sheep, but himself a sheep against the brave."

Such are the conclusions to be drawn from the experience of war against the German fascist invader. What do they show?

They show that we can and must continue to smash the German fascist invaders until they are completely annihilated, until the Soviet land is completely liberated from the Hitler beasts.

Comrades, we are waging a just and patriotic war of liberation. We have no such aims as seizing foreign lands or subjugating foreign peoples. Our aim is clear and noble. We want to rid our Soviet land of the German fascist scum. We want to liberate our brothers, Ukrainians, Moldavians, Byelo-Russians, Latvians, Esthonians, Karelians, from the shame and humiliation to which the Nazi-fascist beasts subject them. To achieve this aim we must smash the German fascist army and annihilate the German invaders to the last man if they do not surrender. There is no other way. This we can do and must do at all costs.

The Red Army possesses everything required to achieve this lofty goal. It lacks only one thing—the ability to use to the full against the enemy the first-class weapons provided by our country. Therefore, the task of the Red Army, its infantrymen, machine-gunners, artillerymen, mortar crews, tankmen, aviators, and cavalrymen is to acquire military knowledge, to study tenaciously, to acquire perfect mastery of weapons, to become experts in their work, and thus learn to strike home at the enemy. Only in this way can the art of defeating the enemy be learned.

Comrades, Red Army men and Red Navy men, commanders and political personnel, men and women guerrilla fighters, in greeting you on May Day, I order:

1. All rank-and-file Red Army men to study the rifle to perfection, to become experts in the use of their weapons and to learn to strike home at the enemy like our glorious snipers who wipe out the German invaders.

2. Machine-gunners, artillerymen, mortar crews, tank men and airmen: Study your weapons to perfection, become experts in your work, strike the German fascist invaders until their complete annihilation.

3. Commanders: Study to perfection the interaction of the various arms, become experts in directing the operations of your troops and show the whole world that the Red Army is capable of fulfilling its great mission of liberation.

4. The entire Red Army: See to it that 1942 becomes the year of the final defeat of the German fascist troops and the liberation of Soviet territory from the Hitler beasts.

5. Men and women guerrilla fighters: Intensify guerrilla warfare behind the German lines, destroy the enemy's communications and transport, destroy enemy headquarters and materiel, spare no bullets against the oppressors of our homeland.

Forward to victory under the unconquerable banner of the great Lenin!

May 1, 1942

THE TWENTY-FIFTH ANNIVERSARY
OF THE OCTOBER REVOLUTION

COMRADES, we are today celebrating the twenty-fifth anniversary of the victory of the Soviet Revolution in our country. Twenty-five years have elapsed since the Soviet system was established in our country. We are now on the threshold of the twenty-sixth year of existence of the Soviet system.

At meetings in celebration of the anniversary of the October Soviet Revolution it is customary to review the work of the government and party bodies in the preceding year. I have been instructed to make such a review for the past year—from November of last year to November of the current year.

The activities of our government and party bodies during the past period proceeded in two directions: in the direction of peaceful construction and the organization of a strong rear for our front, on the one hand; and in the direction of conducting the defensive and offensive operations of the Red Army, on the other.

The peaceful constructive work of our directing bodies in this period consisted in shifting the base of our industry, both war and civilian, to the Eastern regions of our country, in evacuating and installing in their new places industrial workers and plants, in extending crop areas and enlarging the winter crop area in the East and, lastly, in radically improving the operations of our industries which produce supplies for the front and in strengthening labor discipline in the rear, both in the factories and in the collective and state farms. It must be said that this was an extremely difficult and complex large-scale task of organization for all our economic and administrative People's Commissariats, including our railways. Nevertheless, we succeeded in overcoming the obstacles; and now, in spite of all the wartime difficulties, our factories, collective farms, and state farms are undoubtedly working satisfactorily. Our munitions factories and allied enterprises are conscientiously and punctually supplying the Red Army with guns, trench mortars, aircraft, tanks, machine-guns, rifles, and ammunition. Our collective farms and state farms are likewise conscientiously and punctually supplying the population and the Red Army with foodstuffs, and our industry with raw materials. It must be admitted that never before has our country had such a strong and well organized rear.

As a result of all this complex organizational and constructive effort, not only our country, but the people themselves in the rear, have been transformed. They have become more efficient, less slipshod, more disciplined; they have learned to work in wartime fashion, and to realize their duty to our motherland and to her defenders at the front—the Red Army. Bunglers and slackers with no sense of civic duty are becoming fewer and fewer in the rear. The organized and disciplined, those who are imbued with a sense of civic duty, are becoming more and more numerous.

But, as I have said, the past year was not only one of peaceful construction. It was also a year of our Patriotic War against the German invaders, who vilely and treacherously attacked our peaceful country.

As regards the military activities of our directing bodies

during the past year, they consisted in providing for the offensive and defensive operations of the Red Army against the German fascist troops. The hostilities on the Soviet-German Front during the past year may be divided into two periods. The first period was chiefly the winter period, when the Red Army, after repelling the German attack on Moscow, took the initiative, passed to the offensive, drove back the German troops, and in the space of four months advanced, in places, over four hundred kilometers. The second period was the summer period, when the German fascist troops, taking advantage of the absence of a second front in Europe, mustered all their available reserves, pierced the front in the southwestern direction, and, taking the initiative, advanced in places as much as five hundred kilometers in the space of five months.

The hostilities in the first period, especially the Red Army's successful operations in the Rostov, Tula, and Kaluga areas, and at Moscow, Tikhvin, and Leningrad, disclosed two significant facts. They showed, first, that the Red Army and its combatant cadres have become an effective force, not only capable of withstanding the onslaught of the German fascist troops, but also of defeating them in open battle and driving them back. They showed, secondly, that for all their stanchness, the German fascist troops suffer from grave organic defects which, given certain favorable conditions for the Red Army, may lead to their defeat. It is not by mere chance that the German troops, after marching in triumph through all Europe and at one blow smashing the French troops, which had been regarded as first-class troops, met with effective military resistance only in our country; and not only did they meet with resistance, but they were compelled by the blows of the

Red Army to retreat from their positions over four hundred kilometers, abandoning on their line of retreat an immense quantity of guns, machines, and ammunition. This fact cannot be attributed exclusively to the winter conditions of fighting.

The second period of hostilities on the Soviet-German Front was marked by a turn in favor of the Germans, by the initiative passing to the Germans, by the piercing of our front in the southwestern direction, by the advance of the German troops and their reaching the areas of Voronezh, Stalingrad, Novorossiisk, Pyatigorsk, and Mozdok. Taking advantage of the absence of a second front in Europe, the Germans and their allies transferred all their available reserves to the front and, massing them in one direction, the southwestern direction, created a big superiority of forces and achieved substantial tactical gains.

Apparently the Germans are no longer strong enough to conduct a simultaneous offensive in all three directions, in the south, north and center, as was the case in the early months of the German offensive in the summer of last year; but they are still strong enough to organize a serious offensive in some one direction.

What was the main objective of the German fascist strategists when they launched their summer offensive on our front? To judge by the comments of the foreign press, including the German, one might think that the main objective of the offensive was to capture the oil districts of Grozny and Baku. But facts decidedly refute this assumption. Facts show that the German advance towards the oil districts of the U.S.S.R. is not the main, but an auxiliary, objective.

What, then, was the main objective of the German offensive? It was to outflank Moscow from the east; to cut it off from its Volga and Urals rear and then to strike at the city. The German advance southwards, towards the oil districts, had an auxiliary purpose; not only, and not so much, to capture the oil districts as to divert our main reserves to the south and to weaken the Moscow front, and thereby facilitate the success of the blow at Moscow. This, in fact, explains why the main group of the German forces are now in the Orel and the Stalingrad areas, and not in the south.

Recently, an officer of the German general staff fell into the hands of our men. A map was found on this officer showing the plan and schedule of the German troops' advance. From this document it is evident that the Germans intended to be in Borisoglyebsk on July 10, this year, in Stalingrad on July 25, in Saratov on August 10, in Kuibyshev on August 15, in Arzamas on September 10, and in Baku on September 25.

This document fully confirms the information in our possession that the main objective of the German summer offensive was to outflank Moscow from the east and to strike at Moscow; while the object of the advance to the south was, apart from everything else, to divert our reserves as far as possible from Moscow and to weaken the Moscow front so as to facilitate the blow at Moscow. In short, the main objective of the German summer offensive was to surround Moscow and end the war this year.

In November last year the Germans counted on capturing Moscow by a frontal attack, on compelling the Red Army to capitulate and thus bringing the war in the east to a close. These were the illusions with which they sustained their soldiers. As we know, however, these calculations of the Germans miscarried. Having burned their fingers in their attempt at a frontal attack on Moscow last year, the Germans planned to capture Moscow this year by a flanking movement and to end the war in the east in that way. These are the illusions with which they are sustaining their duped soldiers now. As we know, these calculations of the Germans also proved unsound. Their attempt to chase two hares at once—oil and the encirclement of Moscow—landed the German fascist strategists in difficulties.

Thus, the tactical successes of the German summer offensive were not consummated owing to the obvious unfeasibility of their strategical plans.

How are we to explain the fact that the Germans were nevertheless able to take the initiative in military operations this year and achieve substantial tactical successes on our front?

It is to be explained by the fact that the Germans and their allies were able to muster all their available reserves, transfer them to the Eastern front and create a big superiority of forces in one of the directions. There can be no doubt that but for these measures the Germans could not have achieved any success on our front.

But why were they able to muster all their reserves and transfer them to the Eastern front? Because the absence of a second front in Europe enabled them to carry out this operation without any risk.

Hence, the chief reason for the Germans' tactical successes on our front this year is that the absence of a second front in Europe enabled them to transfer to our front all their available reserves and to create a big superiority of forces in the southwestern direction.

Let us assume that there was a second front in Europe as

there was in the first World War, and that this second front diverted, let us say, sixty German divisions and twenty divisions of Germany's allies. What would have been the position of the German troops on our front today? It is not difficult to guess that their position would have been deplorable. More than that, it would have been the beginning of the end of the German fascist troops, for in that case the Red Army would not be where it is now, but somewhere near Pskov, Minsk, Zhitomir, and Odessa. That means that already in the summer of this year the German fascist army would have been on the verge of disaster; and if that did not occur, it was because the Germans were saved by the absence of a second front in Europe.

Let us examine the question of a second front in Europe in its historical aspect.

In the first World War Germany had to fight on two fronts: in the West, chiefly against Great Britain and France, and in the East, against the Russian troops. Thus, in the first World War there was a second front against Germany. Of the 220 divisions which Germany then had, not more than 85 were stationed on the Russian front. If to this we add the troops of Germany's allies then facing the Russian front, namely, 37 Austro-Hungarian divisions, two Bulgarian divisions and three Turkish divisions, we get a total of 127 divisions facing the Russian troops. Most of the remaining divisions of Germany and her allies held the front against the Anglo-French troops, while some of them performed garrison duty in the occupied territories of Europe. Such was the position in the first World War.

What is the position today, in the second World War, in September of this year, let us say?

According to authentic information which is beyond all doubt, of the 256 divisions which Germany now has, no fewer than 179 are on our front. If to this we add 22 Rumanian divisions, 14 Finnish divisions, 10 Italian divisions, 13 Hungarian divisions, one Slovak division and one Spanish division, we get a total of 240 divisions which are now fighting on our front. The remaining divisions of Germany and her allies are performing garrison duty in the occupied countries (France, Belgium, Norway, the Netherlands, Jugoslavia, Poland, Czechoslovakia, etc.), while part of them are fighting in Libya for the possession of Egypt against Great Britain. In all, the Libyan front is diverting four German divisions and 11 Italian divisions.

Hence, instead of 127 divisions as was the case in the first World War, we, today, are facing on our front no less than 240 divisions, and instead of 85 German divisions we have 179 German divisions fighting the Red Army.

This is the chief reason and grounds for the tactical successes the German fascist troops gained on our front this summer.

The German invasion of our country is often compared to Napoleon's invasion of Russia. But this comparison will not bear criticism. Of the 600,000 troops which started out on the march against Russia, Napoleon brought to Borodino barely 130,000, or 140,000. That was all he had at his disposal at Moscow. Well, we now have facing the Red Army over 3,000,000 troops, and troops armed with all the implements of modern warfare. What comparison can there be here?

The German invasion of our country is sometimes also compared to the German invasion of Russia during the first World War. But neither will this comparison bear criticism. First, in the first World War there was the second front in Europe, which made the Germans' position very difficult, whereas in this war there is no second front in Europe. Secondly, in this war, twice as many troops are facing our front as was the case during the first World War. Obviously, the comparison is inappropriate.

You can now imagine how grave and extraordinary are the difficulties that confront the Red Army, and how great is the heroism displayed by the Red Army in its war of liberation against the German fascist invaders.

I think that no other country and no other army could have withstood this onslaught of the savage gangs of German fascist brigands and their allies. Only our Soviet country and only our Red Army are capable of withstanding such an onslaught. And not only withstanding it, but also overpowering it.

It is often asked: But will there be a second front in Europe after all? Yes, there will be; sooner or later, there will be. And there will be one not only because we need it, but above all because our Allies need it no less than we. Our Allies cannot fail to realize that since France has been put out of action, the absence of a second front against fascist Germany may end badly for all the freedom-loving countries, including the Allies themselves.

It may now be regarded as beyond dispute that in the course of the war imposed upon the nations by Hitlerite Germany, a radical demarcation of forces and the formation of two opposite camps have taken place: the camp of the Italo-German coalition, and the camp of the Anglo-Soviet-American coalition.

It is equally beyond dispute that these two opposite coalitions are guided by two different and opposite programs of action.

The program of action of the Italo-German coalition may be characterized by the following points: race hatred; domination of the "chosen" nations; subjugation of other nations and seizure of their territories; economic enslavement of the subjugated nations and spoliation of their national wealth; destruction of democratic liberties; universal institution of the Hitler regime.

The program of action of the Anglo-Soviet-American coalition is: abolition of racial exclusiveness; equality of nations and integrity of their territories; liberation of the enslaved nations and the restoration of their sovereign rights; the right of every nation to manage its affairs in its own way; economic aid to nations that have suffered and assistance in establishing their material welfare; restoration of democratic liberties; destruction of the Hitler regime.

The effect of the program of action of the Italo-German coalition has been that the people in all the occupied countries of Europe—Norway, Denmark, Belgium, the Netherlands, France, Poland, Czechoslovakia, Jugoslavia, Greece, and the occupied regions of the U.S.S.R.—are seething with hatred for the Italo-German tyrants, are causing the Germans and their allies all the damage they can, and are waiting for a favorable opportunity to take revenge on their conquerors for the outrage and violence to which they are subjected.

In this connection, one of the characteristic features of the present situation is the steadily growing isolation of the Italo-German coalition and the depletion of its moral and political reserves in Europe, its growing weakness and disintegration.

The effect of the program of action of the Anglo-Soviet-American coalition has been that the people in all the occupied countries in Europe fully sympathize with the members of this coalition and are prepared to render them all the help of which they are capable.

In this connection, another characteristic feature of the present situation must be noted, namely, that the moral and political reserves of this coalition are growing from day to day in Europe—and not only in Europe—and that this coalition is steadily winning millions of sympathizers who are ready to join it to fight against Hitler's tyranny.

If the relative strength of these two coalitions is examined from the standpoint of human and material resources, the conclusion that one will be forced to arrive at is that the Anglo-Soviet-American coalition has the unquestionable advantage.

But the question is: Is this advantage alone sufficient for victory? As we know, cases occur when resources are abundant, but are expended so inefficiently that the advantage is lost. Obviously, what is needed in addition to resources is ability to mobilize and skill in expending them properly. Is there any reason to doubt that the men of the Anglo-Soviet-American coalition possess this ability and skill? Some people do doubt this. But what grounds have they for their doubts? In the past the men of this coalition have displayed ability and skill in mobilizing the resources of their countries and expending them properly for the purposes of economic, cultural, and political development. What grounds are there, then, for doubting that the men who have displayed skill and ability in mobilizing and distributing resources for economic, cultural and political purposes will prove capable of doing the same for the purpose of prosecuting the war? I think there are no such grounds.

It is said that the Anglo-Soviet-American coalition has every chance of winning, and would certainly win if it did not suffer

66

from an organic defect which might weaken and disintegrate it. This defect, in the opinion of these people, is that this coalition consists of heterogeneous elements having different ideologies, and that this circumstance will prevent them from organizing joint action against the common enemy.

I think that this assertion is wrong.

It would be ridiculous to deny the existence of different ideologies and social systems in the various countries that constitute the Anglo-Soviet-American coalition. But does this preclude the possibility, and the expediency, of joint action on the part of the members of this coalition against the common enemy who threatens to enslave them? Certainly not. More than that. The very existence of this threat imperatively dictates the necessity of joint action among the members of the coalition in order to save mankind from reversion to savagery and medieval brutality. Is not the program of action of the Anglo-Soviet-American coalition a sufficient basis upon which to organize a joint struggle against Hitler tyranny and to vanquish it? I think it is quite sufficient.

These people's assumption is unsound also because it has been utterly refuted by the events of the past year. If these people were right, we should be observing the steady mutual estrangement of the members of the Anglo-Soviet-American coalition. Far from this being the case, however, facts and events point to the steadily growing friendship among the members of the Anglo-Soviet-American coalition and to their amalgamation into a united fighting alliance. Events of the past year supply direct proof of this. In July, 1941, several weeks after Germany attacked the U.S.S.R. Great Britain concluded with us an agreement "on joint action in the war against Germany." At that time we had not yet any agreement with the United States of America on this subject. Ten months later, on May 26, 1942, during Comrade Molotov's visit to Great Britain, the latter concluded with us a "treaty of alliance in the war against Hitlerite Germany and her associates in Europe and on collaboration and mutual aid thereafter." This treaty was concluded for a period of twenty years. It marks a historic turning point in the relations between our country and Great Britain. In June, 1942, during Comrade Molotov's visit to the United States, this country concluded with us an "agreement on the principles applicable to mutual aid in the conduct of the war against aggression," which represented a substantial advance in the relations between the U.S.S.R. and the U.S.A. Lastly, mention must be made of so important a fact as the visit to Moscow of the British Premier, Mr. Churchill, during which complete mutual understanding was reached between the leaders of the two countries. There can be no doubt that all these facts point to the steadily growing friendship between the U.S.S.R., Great Britain, and the United States of America and to their amalgamation into a fighting alliance against the Italo-German coalition.

It follows that the logic of facts is stronger than any other logic.

The only conclusion to be drawn is that the Anglo-Soviet-American coalition has every chance of vanquishing the Italo-German coalition, and that it certainly will do so.

The war has torn down all veils and has laid bare all relationships. The situation has become so clear that nothing is easier than to define our tasks in this war.

In an interview with the Turkish General Erkilet, published in the Turkish newspaper *Gumhuriet,* that cannibal Hitler said: "We shall destroy Russia, so that she will never be able to rise again." This is clear enough, one would think, although it is rather silly. We do not pursue the aim of destroying Germany, for it is impossible to destroy Germany, just as it is impossible to destroy Russia. But we can and must destroy the Hitler state.

Our first task is to destroy the Hitler state and its inspirers.

In the same interview with the same general, that cannibal Hitler went on to say: "We shall continue the war as long as there is an organized military force in Russia." This is clear enough, one would think, although illiterate. We do not pursue the aim of destroying the entire organized military force in Germany, for every literate person will understand that this is not only impossible as regards Germany, just as it is in regard to Russia, but also inadvisable from the point of view of the victor. But we can and must destroy Hitler's army.

Our second task is to destroy Hitler's army and its leaders.

The Hitlerite scoundrels have made it their rule to torture Soviet war prisoners, to slay them by the hundred, and to condemn thousands of them to death by starvation. They outrage and slaughter the civilian population of the occupied territories of our country, men and women, children and the aged, our brothers and sisters. They have set out to enslave or exterminate the population of the Ukraine, Byelorussia, the Baltic Republics, Moldavia, Crimea and the Caucasus. Only villains and scoundrels who are bereft of all honor and who have sunk to the level of brutes can commit such outrages against innocent and unarmed people. But that is not all. They have covered Europe with gallows and concentration camps. They have introduced the vile "hostage system." They shoot and hang absolutely innocent citizens whom they take as "hostages" because some German beast was prevented from raping women or robbing citizens. They have converted Europe into a prison of nations. And this they call the "New Order in Europe." We know the men who are guilty of these outrages, the builders of this "New Order in Europe," all those upstart governor-generals, or just ordinary governors, commandants and sub-commandants. Their names are known to tens of thousands of tormented people. Let these butchers know that they will not escape responsibility for their crimes or elude the hand of retribution of the tormented nations.

Our third task is to destroy the detestable "New Order in Europe" and to punish its builders.

Such are our tasks.

Comrades, we are waging a great war of liberation. We are not waging it alone, but in conjunction with our Allies. It will end in our victory over the vile foes of mankind, over the German fascist imperialists. On its standard is inscribed:

Hail the victory of the Anglo-Soviet-American fighting alliance!

Hail the liberation of the nations of Europe from Hitler's tyranny!

Hail the liberty and independence of our glorious Soviet motherland!

Damnation and death to the German fascist invaders, to their state, their army, their "New Order in Europe"!

Glory to our Red Army! Glory to our Red Navy!

Glory to our men and women guerrilla fighters!

Speech delivered at an anniversary meeting, Moscow, November 6, 1942

THE TWENTY-FIFTH ANNIVERSARY

OF THE OCTOBER REVOLUTION

COMRADES, Red Armymen, commanders and political instructors, men and women guerrilla fighters, working people of the Soviet Union:

On behalf of the Soviet Government and of our Bolshevik Party, I greet you and congratulate you on the twenty-fifth anniversary of the victory of the great October Socialist Revolution.

A quarter of a century ago, under the leadership of the Bolshevik Party and of our great Lenin, the workers and peasants established the Soviet regime in their country. Since then the peoples of the Soviet Union have traversed a glorious road. In the course of these twenty-five years our country grew into a mighty socialist industrial and collective farm power. After winning for themselves freedom and independence, the peoples of the Soviet state united in an indestructible, fraternal commonwealth. The Soviet people freed themselves from all oppression, and by their persevering labors secured for themselves a prosperous and cultured existence.

Today, the peoples of our country are celebrating the twenty-fifth anniversary of the great October Socialist Revolution amidst the conflagration of a fierce struggle against the German fascist invaders and their associates in Europe.

At the beginning of this year, in the winter, the Red Army inflicted severe blows on the German fascist troops. After repelling the German attack on Moscow, it took the initiative, passed to the offensive, and drove the German troops to the West, liberating a number of regions of our country from German slavery. The Red Army thus proved that given certain favorable conditions it can vanquish the German fascist troops.

In the summer, however, the situation at the front changed for the worse. Taking advantage of the absence of a second front in Europe, the Germans and their allies swept together all their reserves, hurled them at our Ukrainian front, and broke through it. At the price of enormous losses the German fascist troops succeeded in advancing on the South, threatening Stalingrad, the Black Sea coast, Grozny, and the approaches to Transcaucasia.

True, the stanchness and courage of the Red Army have thwarted the German plan to outflank Moscow on the East and strike at the capital of our country from the rear. The enemy has been checked at Stalingrad. But although checked at Stalingrad, and having already lost there tens of thousands of men and officers, the enemy is hurling new divisions into the battle and exerting his last efforts. The struggle on the Soviet-German front is becoming increasingly intense. On the outcome of this struggle depend the fate of the Soviet state, the freedom and independence of our country.

Our Soviet people have passed with flying colors the test to which they have been subjected, and are imbued with unshakable confidence in victory. This war has served as a stern test of the strength and durability of the Soviet system. The calculations of the German imperialists that the Soviet state would collapse proved to be utterly baseless. Socialist industry, the collective farm system, the friendship among the nations of our country and the Soviet state have proved to be firm and indestructible. The workers and peasants and the entire intelligentsia of our country, everybody in the rear, are working conscientiously and self-sacrificingly to supply the needs of our armed forces.

The Red Army is bearing the brunt of the war against Hitlerite Germany and its associates. By its self-sacrificing struggle against the fascist armies it has won the love and respect of all the freedom-loving nations of the world. The men and commanders of the Red Army—who had not had sufficient military experience before—have learned to strike the enemy unerring blows, to destroy his manpower and technique, to thwart the enemy's designs and stanchly to defend our towns and villages against the alien invaders. The heroic defenders of Moscow and Tula, of Odessa and Sevastopol, and of Leningrad and Stalingrad have set an example of boundless courage, iron discipline, stanchness and ability to win. Our entire Red Army is following their heroic example. The enemy has already had a taste of the Red Army's power of resistance. It will yet learn the power of the Red Army's crushing blows.

There can be no doubt that the German invaders will plunge into new adventures. But the enemy's forces are already undermined and have now reached the limit. During the course of the war, the Red Army has put out of action over eight million enemy soldiers and officers. The Hitler army, with an admixture of Rumanians, Hungarians, Italians, and Finns, is much weaker than it was in the summer and autumn of 1941.

Comrades, Red Armymen, commanders and political instructors, men and women guerrilla fighters!

The defeat of the German fascist army and the clearing of

our Soviet soil of the Hitler invaders depend upon your tenacity and stanchness, your military skill and readiness to perform your duty to your country!

We can and must clear our Soviet soil of the German scum!
To achieve this we must:

1. Stanchly and stubbornly defend the line of our front, prevent the enemy from advancing any further, do everything to wear the enemy down, exterminate his manpower and destroy his technique;

2. In every way reinforce iron discipline, the strictest order and individual responsibility in our army, perfect the military training of our troops and perseveringly and persistently prepare for a crushing blow at the enemy;

3. Fan the flames of popular guerrilla warfare in the enemy's rear, destroy the enemy's bases, and exterminate the German fascist scoundrels.

Comrades! The enemy has already felt the weight of the Red Army's blows at Rostov, Moscow, and Tikhvin. The day is not far distant when the enemy will again feel the weight of the Red Army's blows. Our turn will come!

Hail the twenty-fifth anniversary of the great October Socialist Revolution!

Long live our Red Army!

Long live our Red Navy!

Long live our brave men and women guerrilla fighters!

Death to the German fascist invaders!

Order of the Day, November 7, 1942

74

THE TWENTY-FIFTH ANNIVERSARY

OF THE FOUNDING OF THE RED ARMY

COMRADES, Red Army and Red Navy men, commanders and political workers, men and women guerrillas:

Today we are celebrating the twenty-fifth anniversary of the existence of the Red Army. A quarter of a century has passed since the Red Army was created. It was created for the struggle against the foreign invaders who strove to enslave our country. February 23, 1918, the day when Red Army detachments utterly routed the troops of the German invaders near Pskov and Narva, was proclaimed the birthday of the Red Army.

In 1918-21, in stubborn struggle against the foreign invaders, the Red Army preserved the honor, freedom, and independence of our Soviet motherland, preserved the right of the peoples of our country to build their life in the way the great Lenin had taught. In the course of two decades the Red Army protected the peaceful, constructive labor of the Soviet people. The peoples of our country never forgot about the encroachments of foreign invaders on our land, and indefatigably strove to enhance the might of the Red Army, supplied it with first-rate combat equipment, and lovingly reared cadres of Soviet warriors.

The Red Army is an army of defense, of peace and friendship among peoples of all countries. It was created not for the conquest of foreign countries, but for the defense of the frontiers of the Soviet country. The Red Army has always treated with respect the rights and independence of all nations.

But in June, 1941, in rude and base violation of the treaty of non-aggression, Hitlerite Germany treacherously attacked our country, and the Red Army found itself compelled to march out to defend its motherland against the German invaders and to oust them from our country. Since that time the Red Army has become an army of life and death struggle with the Hitlerite troops, an army of avengers of the violence and humiliation inflicted by the German fascist scoundrels on our brothers and sisters in the occupied districts of our country.

The Red Army meets the twenty-fifth anniversary of its existence in a decisive moment of the Patriotic War against Hitlerite Germany and her servitors—the Italians, Hungarians, Rumanians, and Finns. For twenty months, the Red Army has been waging a heroic struggle without parallel in history against the invasion of the German fascist hordes. In view of the absence of a second front in Europe, the Red Army alone bears the whole burden of the war. Nevertheless, the Red Army not only stood its own against the onslaught of the German fascist hordes, but in the course of the war has become the terror of the fascist armies.

In the hard battles of the summer and autumn of 1942, the Red Army barred the way to the fascist beasts. Forever will our people preserve the memory of the heroic defense of Sevastopol and Odessa, of the stiff fighting at Moscow and in the foothills of the Caucasus, in the Rzhev area and at Leningrad, of the battle at the walls of Stalingrad, the greatest in the history of wars.

In these great battles our gallant Red Army men, commanders and political workers covered with unfading glory the battle standards of the Red Army and laid a firm foundation for victory over the German fascist armies.

Three months ago Red Army troops began an offensive at the approaches to Stalingrad. Since then the initiative of military operations has been in our hands, while the pace and striking force of the Red Army's offensive operations have not weakened. At present, in the hard conditions of winter, the Red Army advances on a frontage of 1,500 kilometers and achieves success practically everywhere. In the North, at Leningrad; on the Central Front, at the approaches to Kharkov; in the Donbas, at Rostov; on the Azov and Black Sea Coasts, the Red Army strikes one blow after another at Hitler's troops. In three months the Red Army has cleared the enemy from the territory of the Voronezh and Stalingrad Regions, the Checheno-Ingush, North Ossetian, Kabardino-Balkarian, and Kalmyk Autonomous Republics, the Stavropol and Krasnodar Territories, the Cherkess, Karachai and Adygei Autonomous Regions, and nearly all of the Rostov, Kharkov, and Kursk Regions. The expulsion of the enemy from the Soviet country has begun.

What has changed in these three months? Whence such serious reverses of the Germans? What are the causes of these reverses? The balance of forces on the Soviet-German front has changed. The point is that fascist Germany becomes progressively exhausted and weaker while the Soviet Union progressively deploys its reserves and becomes stronger. Time works against fascist Germany.

Hitlerite Germany, which forced the war industry of Europe to work for her, until recently enjoyed superiority over the Soviet Union in equipment, and primarily in tanks and aircraft. This was her advantage. But in twenty months of war the situation has changed. Thanks to the selfless labor of the men and women workers, engineers and technicians of the war industry of the U.S.S.R., the production of tanks, planes, and guns has grown in the course of the war.

During the same time, on the Soviet-German front, the enemy sustained enormous losses in combat equipment, especially in tanks, planes, and guns. During the three months of the Red Army's offensive in the winter of 1942-43 alone, the Germans lost over 7,000 tanks, 4,000 planes, 17,000 guns, and large quantities of other arms. Naturally, the Germans will try to make good these losses, but this will not be so easy to accomplish, as considerable time will be needed for the enemy to be able to repair these enormous losses in equipment. And time does not wait.

Hitlerite Germany began the war against the U.S.S.R. while enjoying numerical superiority in troops already mobilized and ready for battle, compared with the Red Army. This was her advantage. In twenty months, however, the situation has changed in this respect, too. In defensive and offensive battles the Red Army has disabled during the war about 9,000,000 German fascist officers and men, of which number not less than 4,000,000 were killed on the battlefield. The Rumanian, Italian, and Hungarian armies transferred by Hitler to the Soviet-German front have been completely routed.

During the past three months alone the Red Army routed 112 enemy divisions, killing more than 700,000 men and taking over 300,000 prisoners.

The German Command will certainly try to make good these tremendous losses. But, first, the weakness of the German armies is in the shortage of manpower reserves, and consequently it is not known from what sources these losses can be compensated. Secondly, supposing even that by hook and crook the Germans muster up the necessary number of men, time would be needed to gather and train them. And time does not wait.

The Hitlerite army entered the war against the Soviet Union possessing almost two years' experience in conducting large-scale military operations in Europe, with the application of the latest means of warfare. In the initial period of the war the Red Army naturally had not yet and could not have such military experience. This was the advantage of the German fascist army. In twenty months, however, the situation has changed in this respect, too. In the course of the war the Red Army has become a seasoned army. It has learned to strike at the enemy unerringly, taking into consideration his weak and strong sides, as required by modern military science.

Hundreds of thousands and millions of Red Army men have become experts in wielding their arms—rifle, saber, machine gun, and aviation. Tens of thousands of Red Army commanders have become experts in the leading of troops. They have learned to combine personal heroism and courage with skill in directing troops on the battlefield, having discarded the foolish and harmful linear tactics and having firmly adopted the tactics of maneuvering.

One cannot consider fortuitous the fact that the Red Army Command not only liberates Soviet soil from the enemy, but does not let the enemy escape alive from our soil, effecting such serious operations of encirclement and annihilation of enemy armies as may serve as examples of military art. This undoubtedly is an indication of the maturity of our commanders. There can be no doubt that only the correct strategy of the Red Army Command and the flexible tactics of our commanders—its executors—could have resulted in such an outstanding fact as the encirclement and annihilation of the picked army of Germans numbering 330,000 men at Stalingrad.

In this respect, things are far from going well with the Germans. Their strategy is defective because, as a rule, it underestimates the enemy's forces and possibilities and overestimates its own forces. Their tactics follow a routine—they endeavor to fit events at the front into this or that article of the regulations. The Germans are accurate and precise in their actions when the situation permits them to act in the way required by the regulations. In this is their strength. The Germans become helpless when the situation becomes complicated and begins to "run at variance" with this or that article of the regulations, calling for the adoption of an independent decision not provided for by the regulations. In this is their main weakness.

Such are the causes which determined the defeat of the German troops and the successes of the Red Army during the past three months. It does not follow from this, however, that the Hitlerite army has been done for and that it remains only for the Red Army to pursue it to the western frontiers of our country. To think so means to indulge in unwise and harmful self-delusion. To think so means to overestimate our own forces, to underestimate the enemy's forces, and to adopt an adventurous course. The enemy has suffered a defeat, but he is not vanquished as yet.

The German fascist army is now going through a crisis as a result of the blows received from the Red Army. But this does not mean that it cannot recover. The struggle against the German invaders is not yet over—it is just developing and flaring up. It would be foolish to think that the Germans will surrender even one kilometer of our soil without fighting.

The Red Army faces a grim struggle against the perfidious, cruel, and as yet strong enemy. This struggle will require time, sacrifices, the exertion of our forces and the mobilization of all our possibilities. We have begun the liberation of the Soviet Ukraine from the German yoke, but millions of Ukrainians still languish under the yoke of the German enslavers. The German occupationists and their servitors still lord it in Byelorussia, Lithuania, Latvia, and Estonia, in Moldavia, in the Crimea, and in Karelia. Powerful blows have been dealt to the enemy armies, but the enemy has not yet been van-quished. The German invaders offer furious resistance, launch counter-attacks, and try to make a stand on defensive lines. They may embark upon fresh adventures.

This is why there should be no place for complacency, care-lessness, and conceit in our ranks. The whole Soviet people rejoices in the Red Army's victories, but Red Army men, com-manders and political workers should firmly remember the precepts of our teacher Lenin: "The first thing is not to be carried away by victory, and not to become conceited; the second thing is to consolidate the victory; the third thing is to finish off the enemy."

In the name of the liberation of our motherland from the hateful enemy, in the name of final victory over the German fascist invaders, I order:

1. To perfect indefatigably the military training and to strengthen discipline, order, and organization in the whole Red Army and Navy;

2. To deal stronger blows to the enemy troops, to pursue the enemy indefatigably and persistently, without allowing

him to make a stand on defensive lines, not to give him respite day or night, to cut the enemy's communications, to surround the enemy troops and annihilate them if they refuse to down their arms;

3. To fan ever brighter the flames of the guerrilla struggle in the enemy rear, to destroy the enemy's communications, to blow up railway bridges, to thwart the transportation of enemy troops, the supply of arms and ammunition, to blow up and set fire to military stores, to attack the enemy garrisons, to prevent the retreating enemy from burning down our towns and villages, to help the advancing Red Army with all forces and means.

In this lies the pledge of our victory.

Comrades, Red Army and Red Navy men, commanders and political workers, men and women guerrillas! On behalf of the Soviet Government and our Bolshevik Party, I greet and congratulate you on the twenty-fifth anniversary of the Red Army.

Long live our great motherland!

Long live our glorious Red Army, our valiant Navy, our brave men and women guerrillas!

Long live the party of the Bolsheviks, inspirer and organizer of the Red Army's victories!

Death to the German invaders!

Order of the Day, February 23, 1943

MAY DAY, 1943

COMRADES, Red Army and Red Navy men, commanders and political workers, men and women guerrillas, working men and women, men and women peasants, people engaged in intellectual work; brothers and sisters who have temporarily fallen under the yoke of the German oppressors! In the name of the Soviet Government and our Bolshevik Party I greet and congratulate you on the occasion of May First!

The peoples of our country meet May First in the stern days of Patriotic War. They have entrusted their destiny to the Red Army and their hopes have not been misplaced. Soviet warriors stood up resolutely in defense of the motherland, and now for nearly two years have been defending the honor and independence of the peoples of the Soviet Union. During the winter campaign of 1942-43, the Red Army inflicted grave defeats on the Hitlerite troops, annihilated an enormous amount of the enemy's manpower and equipment, surrounded and annihilated two armies of the enemy at Stalingrad, took prisoner over 300,000 enemy officers and men, and liberated hundreds of Soviet towns and thousands of villages from the German yoke.

The winter campaign has demonstrated that the offensive power of the Red Army has grown. Our troops not only hurled the Germans out of the territory the latter had seized in the summer of 1942, but occupied a number of towns and districts which had been in the enemy's hands for about one and a half years.

It proved beyond the Germans' strength to avert the Red Army's offensive. Even for a counter-offensive in a narrow sector of the front in the area of Kharkov the Hitlerite command found itself compelled to transfer more than thirty fresh divisions from Western Europe. The Germans calculated on surrounding Soviet troops in the area of Kharkov and arranging a "German Stalingrad" for our troops. However, the attempt of the Hitlerite Command to take revenge for Stalingrad has collapsed.

Simultaneously the victorious troops of our Allies routed the Italo-German troops in the area of Libya and Tripolitania, cleared these areas of enemies and now continue to batter them in the area of Tunisia, while the valiant Anglo-American aviators strike shattering blows at the military and industrial centers of Germany and Italy, foreshadowing the formation of a second front in Europe against the Italo-German fascists.

Thus, for the first time since the beginning of the war, the blow dealt at the enemy from the east by the Red Army merged with a blow from the west dealt by the troops of our Allies into one joint blow.

All of these circumstances taken together have shaken the Hitlerite war machine to its foundation, have changed the course of the World War, and created the necessary prerequisites for victory over Hitlerite Germany. As a result the enemy was forced to admit a serious aggravation of his position and raised a hue and cry about a military crisis.

True, the enemy tries to disguise his critical situation by clamor about "total" mobilization. But no amount of clamor can do away with the fact that the camp of the fascists is really going through a grave crisis. The crisis in the fascists' camp finds expression in the first place in the fact that the enemy had to renounce openly his original plan of a lightning war. The talk about lightning war is no longer in vogue in the enemy's camp. The vociferous babble about lightning war has yielded place to sad lamentations about the inevitability of protracted war.

While previously the German fascist command boasted of the tactic of the lightning offensive, now this tactic has been discarded and the German fascists boast no more that they effected or intend to effect a lightning offensive, but that they managed to slip away deftly from the flanking blow of the British troops in Northern Africa, or from encirclement by Soviet troops in the area of Demyansk.

The fascist press is replete with boastful reports to the effect that the German troops succeeded in making good their escape from the front and avoided another Stalingrad in one or another sector of the Eastern front or the Tunisian front. Evidently the Hitlerite strategists have nothing else to boast of.

Secondly, the crisis in the fascist camp finds expression in that the fascists begin to speak more frequently about peace. To judge by the reports of the foreign press, one can arrive at the conclusion that the Germans would wish to obtain peace with Britain and the U.S.A. on the condition that the latter two draw away from the Soviet Union, or, on the contrary, they would wish to obtain peace with the Soviet Union under the condition that it draw away from Britain and the U.S.A. Themselves treacherous to the marrow, the German imperialists have the nerve to apply their own yardstick to the Allies, expecting some one of the Allies to swallow the bait.

Obviously it is not from fine living that the Germans babble about peace. The babble about peace in the fascist camp only indicates that they are going through a grave crisis.

But of what kind of peace can one talk with the imperialist bandits from the German fascist camp who have flooded Europe with blood and studded it with gallows? Is it not clear that only the utter routing of the Hitlerite armies and the unconditional surrender of Hitlerite Germany can bring peace to Europe? Is it not because the German fascists sense the coming catastrophe that they babble about peace? The German-Italian fascist camp is experiencing a grave crisis and faces catastrophe.

This does not mean, of course, that the catastrophe of Hitlerite Germany has already come. No, it does not mean that. Hitlerite Germany and her army have been shaken and experience a crisis, but they have not been smashed as yet. It would be naïve to think that the catastrophe will come of itself, drift in with the tide. Another two or three powerful blows from the west and east are needed, such as those dealt to the Hitlerite army in the past five or six months, for the catastrophe of Hitlerite Germany to become an accomplished fact.

For this reason the peoples of the Soviet Union and their Red Army, as well as our Allies and their armies, still face a stern and hard struggle for complete victory over the Hitlerite fiends. This struggle will demand of them great sacrifices, enormous staying power, and iron stanchness. They must mobilize all their forces and possibilities to smash the enemy and thus blaze the road to peace.

Comrades! The Soviet people displays the greatest solicitude for its Red Army. It is ready to give all its forces for the further strengthening of the military might of the Soviet country. In less than four months the peoples of the Soviet Union have donated more than 7,000,000,000 rubles to the Red Army fund. This demonstrates once more that the war against the Germans is truly a national war of all the peoples inhabiting the Soviet Union. Without folding their hands, stanchly and courageously facing the hardships caused by war, workers, collective farmers and intellectuals work at factories and in institutions, on transport, in collective farms and State farms.

But the war against the German fascist invaders demands that the Red Army receive still more guns, tanks, aircraft, machine guns, automatic rifles, trench-mortars, ammunition, equipment, and provisions. Hence it is necessary that the workers, collective farmers, and all Soviet intellectuals work with redoubled energy for the front. It is necessary that all our people and all institutions in the rear work with clockwork efficiency and precision. Let us recall the bequest of great Lenin: "Once war proves inevitable—everything for the war, and the least slackness and lack of energy must be punished by wartime laws."

In return for the confidence and solicitude of its people the Red Army must strike at the enemy still more strongly, exterminate mercilessly the German invaders, drive them incessantly out of the Soviet land.

In the course of the war the Red Army acquired rich military experience. Hundreds of thousands of Red Army men learned to wield their arms to perfection. Many commanders learned skillfully to direct troops on the field of action. But it would be unwise to rest at that. All the Red Army men must learn to wield their arms well, commanders must acquire mastery in the conduct of battle.

But even this is not enough. In military matters, and the more so in such a war as modern war, one cannot stand still. To stop in military matters means to remain behind. And as is known, those who remain behind are beaten. Therefore, the main point now is that the whole Red Army must, day in and day out, perfect its combat training, that all commanders and men of the Red Army must study the experience of war, must learn to fight in such a manner as is needed for the cause of victory.

Comrades, Red Army and Red Navy men, commanders and political workers, men and women guerrillas! While greeting and congratulating you on the occasion of the First of May, I order:

1. That all Red Army men—infantrymen, trench-mortar gunners, artillerymen, tankmen, fliers, sappers, signalmen, and cavalrymen—indefatigably continue to perfect their fighting mastery, to execute precisely the orders of their commanders, the requirements of the Army regulations and instructions, sacredly to observe discipline, and to maintain organization and order.

2. That the commanders of all services and the commanders of combined arms become experts in the leading of troops; skillfully to organize the instruction of all arms and to direct them in battle; to study the enemy, to improve reconnaissance —the eyes and ears of the army—and to remember that without this, one cannot beat the enemy. To raise the efficiency of the work of troops headquarters so that the headquarters of Red Army units and formations become exemplary bodies for the direction of troops; to raise the work of the Army and the rear establishments to the level of requirements presented by modern warfare; to bear firmly in mind that the outcome

of combat operations depends on a full and timely supply of troops with ammunition, equipment, and provisions.

3. That the whole Red Army consolidate and develop the successes of the winter battles; that it does not surrender to the enemy a single inch of our soil; that it be prepared for decisive battles against the German fascist invaders; that in defense it display the stubbornness inherent in the men of our Army; and in the offensive—the resolution, correct interaction of troops and bold maneuver in the field of action, crowned by the encirclement and annihilation of the enemy.

4. That men and women guerrillas strike powerful blows at the enemy's rear establishments, communications, military stores, headquarters and factories; that they destroy the enemy's telegraph and telephone lines; that they draw the wide strata of the Soviet population in the areas captured by the enemy into the active struggle of liberation, and thus save Soviet citizens from extermination by the Hitlerite beasts; that they take merciless revenge on the German invaders for the blood and tears of our wives and children, mothers and fathers, brothers and sisters; that they help, by all means, the Red Army in its struggle against the base Hitlerite enslavers.

Comrades! The enemy has already felt the weight of the shattering blows of our troops. The time is approaching when the Red Army, together with the armies of our Allies, will break the backbone of the fascist beast.

Long live our glorious motherland!
Long live our valiant Red Army! Long live the Red Navy!
Long live our gallant men and women guerrillas!
Death to the German invaders!

Order of the Day, May 1, 1943

THE TWENTY-SIXTH ANNIVERSARY

OF THE OCTOBER REVOLUTION

COMRADES! Today the peoples of the Soviet Union celebrate the twenty-sixth anniversary of the great October Socialist Revolution. For the third time our country marks the anniversary of her people's revolution in the conditions of the Patriotic War.

In October, 1941, our motherland lived through hard days. The enemy approached the capital. He surrounded Leningrad from the land. Our troops were compelled to retreat. Enormous efforts of the army and the exertion of all the forces of the people were necessary to check the enemy and to strike a serious blow at him at Moscow.

By October, 1942, the danger to our motherland had become even greater. The enemy stood then barely one hundred and twenty kilometers from Moscow, had broken into Stalingrad, and entered the foothills of the Caucasus.

But even in those grave days the army and the people did not lose heart, but stanchly bore all trials. They found strength to check the enemy and to deal him a retaliating blow. True to the behests of our great Lenin, they defended the achievements of the October Revolution without sparing their strength and their lives.

As is well known, those efforts of the army and the people were not in vain. Shortly after the October days of last year our troops passed over to the offensive and struck a fresh powerful blow at the Germans, first at Stalingrad, in the Caucasus, in the area of the middle reaches of the Don, and then, at the beginning of 1943, at Velikie Luki, at Leningrad, and in the area of Rhzev and Vyazma. Since then the Red Army has never let the initiative out of its hands. Its blows throughout the summer of this year became increasingly strong, its military mastery grew with every month. Since then our troops have won big victories and the Germans have suffered one defeat after another.

No matter how hard the enemy tried he still failed to score any success on the Soviet-German front that was of the least importance.

1. A YEAR OF RADICAL TURN IN THE COURSE OF THE WAR

The past year, between the twenty-fifth and twenty-sixth anniversaries of the October Revolution, marked a turn in the Patriotic War. This year marked a turn, in the first place, because in this year the Red Army, for the first time during the course of the war, succeeded in carrying through a big summer offensive against the German troops, and under the blows of our forces the German fascist troops were compelled to abandon hurriedly the territory they had seized, not infrequently saving themselves from encirclement by flight and abandoning on the battlefield huge quantities of equipment, stores of armaments and ammunition, and large numbers of wounded officers and men.

Thus the successes of our summer campaign in the second half of this year followed up and completed the successes of our winter campaign at the beginning of this year.

Now, when the Red Army is developing the successes of the winter campaign and has dealt a powerful blow at German troops in summer, it is possible to consider as finally dead and buried the fairy tale that the Red Army is allegedly incapable of conducting a successful offensive in the summertime. The past year has shown that the Red Army can advance in summer just as well as in winter.

As a result of these offensive operations in the course of the past year our troops were able to fight their way forward from 500 kilometers in the central part of the front up to 1,300 kilometers in the south and to liberate nearly 1,000,000 square kilometers of territory—that is, almost two-thirds of the Soviet land temporarily seized by the enemy.

Along with this the enemy troops have been hurled back from Vladikavkaz to Kherson, from Elista to Krivoi Rog, from Stalingrad to Kiev, from Voronezh to Gomel, from Vyazma and Rzhev to the approaches of Orsha and Vitebsk.

Having no faith in the stability of their earlier successes on the Soviet-German front, the Germans had been building powerful defense lines for a long time beforehand, especially along the big rivers. But in this year's battles neither rivers nor powerful fortifications saved the Germans. Our troops shattered the Germans' defense and within only three months of the summer of 1943 skillfully forced four very serious water barriers—the Northern Donets, the Desna, the Sozh, and the Dnieper. I do not speak even about such barriers as the Germans' defense in the area of the Mius River—west of Rostov—and the defense in the area of the Molochnaya River —near Melitopol. At present the Red Army is battering the enemy successfully on the other side of the Dnieper.

This year also marked a turn, because the Red Army within

a comparatively short time was able to annihilate and grind down the most experienced old cadres of German fascist troops, and at the same time to steel and multiply its own cadres in successful offensive battles in the course of the year.

In the battles on the Soviet-German front during the past year the German-fascist army lost more than 4,000,000 officers and men, including not less than 1,800,000 killed. During this year the Germans also lost more than 14,000 aircraft, over 25,000 tanks, and not less than 40,000 guns.

The German fascist army now is not what it was at the outbreak of war. While at the outbreak of war it had sufficient numbers of experienced cadres, now it has been diluted with newly baked, young, inexperienced officers whom the Germans are hurriedly throwing onto the front, as they have neither the necessary reserves of officers nor the time to train them.

The picture presented today by the Red Army is quite different. Its cadres have grown and been tempered in successful offensive battles in the course of the past year. The numbers of its fighting cadres are growing and will grow further as the existence of the necessary officer reserve gives it time and opportunity to train young officer cadets and promote them to responsible posts.

It is characteristic that instead of the 240 divisions which faced our front last year, 179 of which were German divisions, this year the Red Army at the front is faced with 257 divisions, of which 207 are German. The Germans evidently count upon compensating for the lower quality of their divisions by increasing their numbers. However, the defeat of the Germans in the past year shows that it is impossible to compensate for

93

deterioration in the quality of divisions by increasing their numbers.

From a purely military point of view the defeat of the German troops on our front at the close of this year was predetermined by two major events: the battle of Stalingrad and the battle of Kursk.

The battle of Stalingrad ended in the encirclement of a German army 300,000 strong, its rout and the capture of about one-third of the surrounded troops. To form an idea of the scale of that slaughter unparalleled in history which took place on the fields of Stalingrad, one should know that after the battle of Stalingrad was over, there were found and buried 147,200 dead German officers and men and 46,700 dead Soviet officers and men.

Stalingrad signified the decline of the German fascist army. As is well known, the Germans were unable to recover after the Stalingrad slaughter.

As to the battle of Kursk, it ended in the rout of the two main advancing groups of German fascist troops, and in our troops launching a counter-offensive which turned subsequently into the powerful summer offensive of the Red Army.

The battle of Kursk began with the offensive of the Germans on Kursk from the north and south. That was the last attempt of the Germans to carry out a big summer offensive and in the event of its success to redeem their losses. As is well known, the offensive ended in failure. The Red Army not only repulsed the German offensive, but passed over to the offensive itself and by a series of consecutive blows in the course of the summer period hurled back the German fascist troops beyond the Dnieper. If the battle of Stalingrad foreshadowed the decline of the German fascist army, the battle of Kursk confronted it with disaster.

Finally, this year marked a turn, because the successful offensive of the Red Army radically aggravated the economic and military-political situation of fascist Germany and confronted her with a profound crisis. The Germans counted on carrying out in the summer of this year a successful offensive on the Soviet-German front to redeem their losses and to bolster their shaken prestige in Europe. But the Red Army upset the Germans' calculations, repulsed their offensive, launched an offensive itself, and proceeded to drive the Germans westward and thereby crushed the prestige of German arms.

The Germans counted on taking the line of prolonging the war, started building defense lines and "walls," and proclaimed for all to hear that their new positions were impregnable. But the Red Army again upset the Germans' calculations, broke through their defense lines and "walls," and continues to advance successfully, giving them no time to drag out the war.

The Germans counted on rectifying the situation at the front by "total" mobilization. But here, too, events upset the Germans' calculations. The summer campaign has already consumed two-thirds of the "totally" mobilized men; however, it does not look as if this circumstance has brought about any improvement in the position of the German fascist army.

It may prove necessary to proclaim another "total" mobilization, and there is no reason why a repetition of such a measure should not result in the "total" collapse of a certain state.

The Germans counted on retaining a firm hold on the

Ukraine in order to avail themselves of the Ukrainian agricultural produce for their army and population, and of the Donbas coal for the factories and railways serving the German army. But here, too, they miscalculated. As a result of the successful offensive of the Red Army the Germans have lost not only the Donbas coal but also the richest grain-growing regions of the Ukraine, and there is no reason to think that they will not lose the rest of the Ukraine, too, in the nearest future.

Naturally all these miscalculations could not but impair and in fact did impair radically the economic and military-political situation of fascist Germany. Fascist Germany experiences a profound crisis. She faces disaster.

2. NATIONWIDE ASSISTANCE TO THE FRONT

The successes of the Red Army would have been impossible without the support of the people, without the selfless work of the Soviet people in the factories and plants, collieries and mines, in transport and agriculture.

In hard wartime conditions the Soviet people proved able to insure its army everything most necessary and constantly perfected its fighting equipment. Never during the whole course of the war has the enemy been able to surpass our army as regards quality of armaments. At the same time, our industry has supplied the front with ever greater quantities of fighting equipment.

The past year marked a turn not only in the progress of hostilities, but also in the work of our rear. We were no longer confronted with such tasks as evacuating enterprises to the east and of switching industry to the production of armaments. The Soviet state now has an efficient and rapidly expanding war economy.

Thus all the efforts of the people could be concentrated on the increase of production and on the further improvement of armaments, especially of tanks, aircraft, guns, and self-propelling artillery. In this we have gained big successes. Supported by the entire people, the Red Army received uninterrupted supplies of fighting equipment, rained millions of bombs, mines, and shells upon the enemy, brought thousands of tanks and aircraft into battle.

There is every ground to say that the selfless labor of Soviet people in the rear will go down in history along with the heroic struggle of the Red Army as an unexampled feat of people in defense of their motherland. The workers of the Soviet Union who in the years of peaceful construction built up a highly developed, powerful socialist industry, have during this Patriotic War been working with a real fury of energy to help the front, displaying true labor heroism.

Everyone knows that in the war against the U.S.S.R. the Hitlerites had at their disposal not only the highly developed industry of Germany, but also the rather powerful industries of the vassal and occupied countries. Nevertheless the Hitlerites failed to maintain the quantitative superiority in military equipment which they had at the outbreak of the war against the Soviet Union. Now the former superiority of the enemy as regards the number of tanks, aircraft, mortars, and automatic rifles has been eliminated. If our army now experiences no serious shortage of arms, ammunition, and equipment, credit for this goes in the first place to our working class.

The peasants of the Soviet Union who during the year of peaceful construction, on the basis of the collective farming system, transformed backward farming into up-to-date agriculture, have displayed during the Patriotic War a high degree of understanding of the common national interest which has no parallel in the history of the countryside. By selfless labor to help the front they have shown that the Soviet peasantry considers this war against the Germans its own cause, a war for its own life and liberty.

It is well known that as a result of its invasion by the fascist hordes our country was deprived temporarily of the important agricultural districts of the Ukraine, of the Don and the Kuban valleys. Nevertheless, our collective and state farms supplied the army and the country with food without any serious interruptions.

Naturally, without the collective farming system, without the selfless labor of the men and women collective farmers, we could not have coped with this most difficult task. If in the third year of the war our army experiences no shortage of food, if the population is supplied with food, and industry with raw materials, this is evidence of the strength and vitality of our collective farming system and of the patriotism of our collective farm peasantry.

A great part in helping the front has been played by our transport, by railway transport in the first place, and also by river, sea, and motor transport. As is known, transport is a vital means of communication between the rear and the front. One may manufacture great quantities of arms and ammunition, but if transport does not deliver them to the front in time they may remain a dead weight as far as the front is concerned. It must be said that transport plays a decisive part in the timely delivery to the front of arms, ammunition, food, clothing, etc.

And if in spite of wartime difficulties and shortages of fuel, we have been able to supply the front with everything necessary, this should be credited in the first place to our transport workers and employees.

Nor does our intelligentsia lag behind the working class and peasantry in helping the front. The Soviet intelligentsia is working with devotion for the defense of our country, constantly improving the armaments of the Red Army, and the technology and organization of production. It helps the workers and collective farmers to expand industry and agriculture, and promotes Soviet science and culture in the conditions of war. This does credit to our intelligentsia.

All the peoples of the Soviet Union have risen as one to defend their motherland, rightly considering the present Patriotic War the common cause of all working people, irrespective of nationality or religion.

By now the Hitlerite politicians have themselves seen how hopelessly stupid were their hopes of discord and strife among the peoples of the Soviet Union. The friendship of the peoples of our country has withstood all hardships and trials of war and has become tempered still further in the common struggle of all Soviet people against the fascist invaders.

This is a source of the strength of the Soviet Union.

As in the years of peaceful construction, so in the days of war, the leading and guiding force of the Soviet people has been the party of Lenin, the party of the Bolsheviks. No other party has ever enjoyed or enjoys such prestige among the masses of the people as our Bolshevik Party.

And this is natural. Under the leadership of the party of the Bolsheviks the workers, peasants, and intelligentsia of our country have won their freedom and built a socialist society.

99

In this Patriotic War the party stood before us as the inspirer and organizer of the nationwide struggle against the fascist invaders.

The organizational work of the party has united and directed toward a common goal all the efforts of the Soviet people, subordinating all our forces and means to the cause of the enemy's defeat. During the war the party has cemented still further its kinship with the people, has established still closer connections with the broad masses of the working people. This is a source of strength for our state.

The present war has forcefully confirmed Lenin's well-known statement that war is an all-around test of a nation's material and spiritual forces. The history of wars teaches that only those states stood this test which proved stronger than their adversaries as regards the development and organization of their economy, as regards the experience, skill, and fighting spirit of their troops, and as regards the fortitude and unity of their people throughout the war.

Ours is just such a state. The Soviet state was never so stable and solid as now in the third year of the Patriotic War. The lessons of the war show that the Soviet system proved not only the best form of organizing the economic and cultural development of the country in the years of peaceful construction, but also the best form of mobilizing all the forces of the people for resistance to the enemy in time of war.

The Soviet power set up twenty-six years ago has transformed our country within a short historical period into an impregnable fortress. The Red Army has the most stable and reliable rear of all the armies in the world. This is a source of the strength of the Soviet Union.

There is no doubt that the Soviet state will emerge from the war even stronger and even more consolidated. The German invaders are desolating and devastating our lands in an endeavor to undermine the power of our state. To an even greater extent than before, the offensive of the Red Army has exposed the barbarous bandit nature of the Hitlerite army. In the districts they seized the Germans have exterminated hundreds of thousands of our civilians. Like the medieval barbarians of Attila's hordes, the German fiends trample the fields, burn down villages and towns, and demolish industrial enterprises and cultural institutions.

The German crimes are evidence of the weakness of the fascist invaders, for only usurpers who themselves do not believe in their victory act in this way. And the more hopeless the position of the Hitlerites becomes, the more viciously they rage in their atrocities and plunder.

Our people will not forgive the German fiends for these crimes. We shall make the German criminals answer for all their misdeeds.

In areas where the fascist cutthroats have for a time been masters we shall have to restore the demolished towns and villages, industry, transport, agriculture, and cultural institutions; we shall have to create normal living conditions for the Soviet people delivered from fascist slavery. The work of the restoration of the economy and culture is already going full blast in the districts liberated from the enemy. But this is only the beginning.

We must completely eliminate the consequences of the Germans' domination in the districts liberated from German occupation. This is the great national task. We can and must cope with this difficult task within a short time.

3. CONSOLIDATION OF THE ANTI-HITLER COALITION. DISINTEGRATION OF THE FASCIST BLOC

The past year has marked a turn not only in the Patriotic War of the Soviet Union but in the whole World War. The changes which have taken place during this year in the military and international situation have been favorable to the U.S.S.R. and the Allied countries friendly to it, and detrimental to Germany and her accomplices in brigandage in Europe.

The victories of the Red Army have had results and consequences far beyond the limits of the Soviet-German front; they have changed the whole further course of the World War and acquired great international significance. The victory of the Allied countries over the common enemy has come nearer, while the relations among the Allies, the fighting partnership of their armies, far from weakening have, contrary to the expectations of their enemies, grown stronger and more enduring.

Eloquent evidence of this also are the historic decisions of the Moscow conference of representatives of the Soviet Union, Great Britain and the United States of America recently published in the press. Now our united countries are filled with determination to deal the enemy common blows which will result in final victory over him.

This year the Red Army's blows at the German fascist troops were supported by the combat operations of our Allies in North Africa, in the Mediterranean Basin and in southern Italy. At the same time the Allies subjected and are still subjecting important industrial centers of Germany to substantial bombing and thus considerably weakening the enemy's military power. If to all this is added the fact that the Allies are regularly supplying us with various munitions and raw materials, it can be said without exaggeration that by all this they considerably facilitated the successes of our summer campaign.

Of course the present actions of the Allied armies in the south of Europe cannot as yet be regarded as a second front. But still this is something like a second front. Obviously the opening of a real second front in Europe, which is not so distant, will considerably hasten the victory over Hitlerite Germany and will consolidate even more the fighting partnership of the Allied countries.

Thus the events of the past year show that the anti-Hitler coalition is a firm association of peoples, and rests on a solid foundation.

By now it is obvious to everyone that by unleashing this war the Hitlerite clique has led Germany and her flunkeys into a hopeless impasse. The defeats of the fascist troops on the Soviet-German front and the blows of our Allies at the Italo-German troops have shaken the whole edifice of the fascist bloc, and it is crumbling now before our very eyes. Italy has dropped out of the Hitlerite coalition never to return. Mussolini can change nothing because he is in fact a prisoner of the Germans.

Next in line are the other partners in the coalition. Finland, Hungary, Rumania, and other vassals of Hitler, discouraged by Germany's military defeats, have now finally lost faith in an outcome of the war favorable for them, and are anxious to find a way out of the bog into which Hitler has dragged them. Now, when the time has come to answer for their brigandage, Hitlerite Germany's accomplices in plunder but recently so obedient to their master are in search of a vent, looking for an opportune moment to slip out of the bandit gang unnoticed.

In entering the war the partners in the Hitlerite bloc counted on a quick victory. They had already allotted beforehand who would get what: who would get buns and pies and who bumps and black eyes. They naturally meant the bumps and black eyes for their adversaries, and the buns and pies for themselves. But now it is obvious that Germany and her flunkeys will get no buns and pies, but will have to share the bumps and black eyes.

Anticipating this unattractive prospect, Hitler's accomplices are now racking their brains for a way to get out of the war with as few bumps and black eyes as possible. Italy's example shows Hitler's vassals that the longer they postpone their inevitable break with the Germans and permit them to lord it in their states, the greater the devastation in store for their countries, the more suffering their peoples will have to bear. Italy's example also shows that Hitlerite Germany has no intention of defending her vassal countries, but means to convert them into a scene of devastating war if only she can stave off the hour of her own defeat.

The cause of German fascism is lost, and the sanguinary "new order" it has set up is on the way to collapse. An outburst of the people's wrath against the fascist enslavers is brewing in the occupied countries of Europe. Germany's former prestige in the countries of her Allies and in the neutral countries is lost beyond recovery, and her economic and political ties with neutral states have been undermined. The time is long past when the Hitlerite clique clamored boisterously about the Germans winning world domination. Now, as is well known, the Germans have other matters than world domination to worry about, they have to think about keeping body and soul together.

Thus the course of the war has shown that the alliance of fascist states did not and does not rest on a reliable foundation. The Hitlerite coalition was formed on the basis of the predatory, rapacious ambitions of its members. As long as the Hitlerites were scoring military successes, the fascist coalition seemed to be a stable association. But the very first defeats of the fascist troops resulted in the actual disintegration of the bandit bloc.

Hitlerite Germany and her vassals stand on the verge of disaster.

The victory of the Allied countries over Hitlerite Germany will put on the agenda the important questions of the organizing and rebuilding of the state, economic and cultural life of the European peoples. The policy of our government in these questions remains unchanging. Together with our Allies we shall have to:

1. Liberate the peoples of Europe from the fascist invaders and help them rebuild their national states dismembered by the fascist enslavers; the peoples of France, Belgium, Yugoslavia, Czechoslovakia, Poland, Greece, and other states now under the German yoke must again become free and independent;

2. Grant the liberated peoples of Europe the full right and freedom to decide for themselves the question of their form of government;

3. Take measures that all fascist criminals responsible for this war and the sufferings of the peoples bear stern punish-

ment and retribution for all the crimes they committed, no matter in what country they may hide;

4. Establish such an order in Europe as will completely preclude the possibility of new aggression on the part of Germany;

5. Establish lasting economic, political, and cultural collaboration among the peoples of Europe based on mutual confidence and mutual assistance for the purpose of rehabilitating the economic and cultural life destroyed by the Germans.

During the past year the Red Army and the Soviet people have achieved great successes in the struggle against the German invaders. We achieved a radical turning point in the war in favor of our country, and now the war is heading for its final outcome.

But it is not like the Soviet people to rest on their achievements, to exult in their successes. Victory may elude us if complacency appears in our ranks. Victory cannot be won without struggle and strain. It is won in battle. Victory is near now, but to win it a fresh exertion of strength is needed, selfless work throughout the rear, skillful and resolute actions of the Red Army at the front.

It would be a crime against the motherland, against the Soviet people who have fallen temporarily under the fascist yoke, against the peoples of Europe languishing under German oppression, if we failed to use all opportunities to hasten the enemy's defeat. The enemy must not be given any respite. That is why we must exert all our strength to finish off the enemy.

The Soviet people and the Red Army clearly see the difficulties of the coming struggle. But now it is already clear that the day of our victory is approaching. The war has entered that stage when it is a question of driving the invaders completely from Soviet soil and liquidating the fascist "new order in Europe." The time is not far distant when we shall completely clear the enemy from the Ukraine and Byelorussia and the Leningrad and Kalinin Regions, liberate from the German invaders the peoples of the Crimea, Lithuania, Latvia, Estonia, Moldavia, and the Karelo-Finnish Republic.

Comrades! For the victory of the Anglo-Soviet-American fighting alliance! For the liberation of the peoples of Europe from the fascist yoke! For the complete expulsion of the German fiends from our land!

Long live our Red Army!
Long live our Navy!
Long live our gallant men and women guerrillas!
Long live our great motherland!
Death to the German invaders!

Speech delivered at Moscow, November 6, 1943

THE TWENTY-SIXTH ANNIVERSARY

OF THE OCTOBER REVOLUTION

COMRADES, Red Army and Navy men, sergeants, officers and generals, men and women guerrillas! Working people of the Soviet Union! On behalf of the Soviet government and of our Bolshevik Party I greet and congratulate you on the twenty-sixth anniversary of the great October Socialist Revolution.

We are celebrating the twenty-sixth anniversary of our great socialist revolution at a time of glorious victories scored by the Red Army over the enemies of our country. For over two years now our people have been waging a war of liberation against the German fascist subjugators. One year ago our homeland was experiencing grim days. The enemy had at that time seized a large part of our territory. Millions of Soviet people were languishing in German bondage. The enemy hordes were pressing toward the Volga to turn Moscow from the east; they were besetting the approaches to Transcaucasia.

But with the very bodies of its men the Red Army barred the enemy's way. Our troops halted the hordes of foreign marauders and after routing them at Stalingrad began to drive them rapidly to the west. Without exception the Red Army has ever since held the initiative of operations in its hands.

In the winter of 1942-43 our gallant troops routed the crack German, Italian, Rumanian, and Hungarian armies, killed or captured over a million officers and men, and liberated a vast territory covering up to half a million square kilometers.

In the summer of 1943 the Red Army dealt the enemy another staggering blow. In the space of a few days our forces frustrated the German summer offensive and by so doing buried Hitler's plan of defeating the main forces of the Red Army and turning Moscow from the Orel and Kursk side. Moreover, the Red Army itself went over to a determined offensive, broke up the enemy's powerful defense zones, and in the space of three months drove him back to the west, at some points for four hundred to five hundred kilometers.

In the course of the summer campaign our forces ejected the enemy from the whole of the Ukraine east of the Dnieper, from the Donbas, Taman, Orel, and Smolensk Regions, entered the Ukraine west of the Dnieper, captured Kiev, capital of the Soviet Ukraine, and also entered Byelorussia, captured the approaches to the Crimea and liberated over 160 towns and over 38,000 inhabited localities.

In the past year the Red Army has recovered from the Germans nearly two-thirds of our territory previously seized by the Germans and has delivered tens of millions of Soviet citizens from the German yoke. In the past year the Germans have lost on the Soviet-German front over 4,000,000 officers and men, including at least 1,800,000 killed. On the Soviet-German front the crack cadre divisions of the German fascist army have met their inglorious end; and together with them Hitler's plans of conquering the world and subjugating nations have been buried for all time.

True, the German army is still fighting stubbornly, it is clinging to every position. But the reverses the Germans have sustained since the defeat of their forces at Stalingrad have undermined the fighting spirit of the German army. Today the Germans dread encirclement like the very plague, and when in danger of being outflanked by our forces they flee, abandoning their equipment and their wounded on the field.

In the offensive operations of the past year our forces have gained experience in modern warfare. Our officers and generals are ably directing their troops, they are successfully mastering the art of military leadership. The Red Army has become the most powerful, most tempered of modern armies. The Red Army's victories have further consolidated the international position of the Soviet Union.

Our army's offensive has been supported by the operations of the Allied forces in North Africa, in the Italian islands and in the south of Italy. The air forces of our Allies have subjected Germany's industrial centers to telling bombing attacks.

There is no doubt that the Red Army's blows at the German forces from the East, seconded by the blows dealt by the main Allied forces from the West, will crush the military might of Hitler Germany and result in the complete victory of the anti-Hitler coalition.

The Red Army could not have achieved this year's great victories without the aid rendered to the front by the whole people. The Soviet people are giving all their efforts to support their army. An endless stream of arms, ammunition, provisions, and equipment is flowing to the front. The Urals and the Kuznetsk Basin, the Moscow and Volga country, Leningrad and Baku, Kazakhstan and Uzbekistan, Georgia and Armenia—all of our republics and regions have come to be a mighty Red Army arsenal.

The Soviet people are successfully rehabilitating the industrial and agricultural areas recaptured from the enemy, rebuilding the factories, mills, mines, and railways, restoring the state and collective farms and enlisting the Soviet forces in the liberated areas to serve the front.

Our successes are indeed great. But to rest content with the successes we have achieved so far would be naïve. Today, when the Red Army is battering the enemy beyond the Dnieper and is pressing forward to our country's western frontiers, it would be particularly dangerous to lapse into self-satisfied complacency and to underrate the grave difficulties of the struggle that still lies ahead. The enemy is now going to fight more viciously than ever for every scrap of territory he has seized.

Our army's advance hastens the hour of reckoning with the Germans for the crimes they have committed on our soil. The struggle for final victory over the German-fascist invaders will call for still greater exertion and more deeds of valor on the part of our Army and our people.

Comrades, Red Army and Navy men, sergeants, officers, and generals, men and women guerrillas! You have scored great victories in the titanic battles against our mortal enemy and have covered the battle standards of the Red Army and Navy with unfading glory. The Red Army and Navy now enjoy every opportunity to clear the whole Soviet land of the German invaders in the near future.

In the name of our country's victory over the German fascist fiends I hereby order:

1. All our rank and file and sergeants tirelessly to improve their fighting efficiency, to observe strictly the regulations and orders of commanders and superiors, and everywhere and always to maintain exemplary order, firm discipline, and a high degree of organization;

2. Officers and generals of all arms of the service to improve continually their direction of troops in action and the co-ordination of all arms, to consolidate the successes of the offensive, effectively to follow in swift pursuit of the enemy's forces, to bring up their rear services faster and to be bolder in using their reserves for fresh blows;

3. The whole of the Red Army boldly and resolutely to break up the enemy's defenses, to pursue the enemy day and night, giving him no chance to entrench on intermediate lines, to cut the enemy's communications by able and daring maneuvering, to surround and split up the enemy's forces and to annihilate or capture his men and materiel;

4. Men and women guerrillas to rouse the Soviet people to armed struggle against the Germans, to increase by every means their assistance to the Red Army in its advance, to wreck the enemy's rear services and headquarters, to save Soviet citizens from being killed or sent to servitude in Germany, and ruthlessly to exterminate the German fascist blackguards.

Men of the Red Army and Navy, men and women guerrillas! Forward to the complete defeat of the German fascist invaders!

Long live the twenty-sixth anniversary of the great October Socialist Revolution!

Long live our victorious Red Army!

Long live our victorious Navy!

Long live our gallant men and women guerrillas!

Long live our great motherland!

Death to the German invaders!

Order of the Day, November 7, 1943

THE TWENTY-SIXTH ANNIVERSARY

OF THE FOUNDING OF THE RED ARMY

COMRADES, Red Army men and Red Navy men, sergeants, officers and generals, men and women guerrillas! The peoples of our country meet the twenty-sixth anniversary of the Red Army in the midst of the historical victories of Soviet troops over the German fascist troops. For over a year the Red Army has been conducting a victorious offensive, battering the armies of the Hitlerite invaders and sweeping them off Soviet soil. During this period the Red Army successfully carried out the winter campaign of 1942-43, won the summer battles of 1943, and developed the victorious winter offensive of 1943-44.

In these campaigns without parallel in the history of wars, the Red Army made a fighting advance to the west of up to 1,700 kilometers at places and cleared the enemy from nearly three-fourths of the Soviet territory he had captured.

In the course of the present winter campaign the Red Army liquidated the powerful defense of the Germans all along the Dnieper, from Zhlobin to Kherson, and thereby upset the Germans' calculations on the successful conduct of protracted defensive war on the Soviet-German front.

Within the three months of the winter campaign our gallant troops have won most important victories on the territories of the Ukraine west of the Dnieper; completed the liberation of the Kiev, Dniepropetrovsk, and Zaporozhye Regions; liberated the entire Zhitomir Region and almost the whole of the Rovno and Kirovograd Regions, as well as a number of districts of the Vinnitsa, Nikolayev, Kamenetz-Podolsk, and Volynia Regions. By resolute actions the Red Army liquidated the attempts of a German counter-offensive in the Zhitomir, Krivoi Rog, and Uman areas. Soviet troops arranged a new Stalingrad for the Germans west of the Dnieper by surrounding and wiping out ten German divisions and one brigade in the Korsun-Shevchenkovsky area.

A great victory has been won by Soviet troops at Leningrad. Our troops broke the powerful system of permanent, deeply echeloned fortifications of the enemy, routed a strong grouping of German troops and completely freed Leningrad from enemy blockade and barbarous shellings. Soviet soldiers are completing the clearing of the Leningrad and Kalinin Regions of the fascist fiends and have set foot on the soil of Soviet Estonia. The mass expulsion of the occupationists from Soviet Byelorussia is under way: the Gomel and Polessye Regions have been nearly entirely liberated, as has been a number of districts of the Mogilev and Vitebsk Regions.

Under the unfavorable conditions of the present winter, having overcome the powerful defensive zones of the enemy, our troops within the three months of the winter campaign cleared of the invaders about 200,000 square kilometers of Soviet soil. The Red Army recaptured from the enemy over 13,000 inhabited localities, including 82 towns and 320 railway stations. New millions of Soviet citizens have been delivered from fascist captivity. Important agricultural and industrial areas with the richest resources of iron ore and manganese have been restored to our motherland. The Germans have lost these economically important areas to which they clung so desperately.

Now it is probably already obvious to everyone that Hitlerite Germany is irresistibly heading for catastrophe. True, the conditions for the prosecution of war in the present war are more favorable for Germany than during the last World War, when from the very beginning to the end of the war she waged a struggle on two fronts. However, a great drawback for Germany is the fact that in this war the Soviet Union proved to be much stronger than old Tsarist Russia was in the last war.

In the First World War six great powers—France, Russia, Great Britain, the United States of America, Japan and Italy—fought on two fronts against the German bloc. In the present war Italy and Japan went over to Germany's side, Finland joined the fascist bloc, Rumania who in the last war fought against Germany passed over, and up to the present Germany's main forces are still engaged on one front against the Soviet Union.

It is known from history that Germany always won a war when she fought on one front and, on the contrary, lost a war when she was forced to fight on two fronts. In the present war Germany, though fighting with her main forces on one front against the U.S.S.R., nevertheless not only proved unable to score a victory but has been placed on the verge of disaster by the powerful blows of the armed forces of the Soviet Union. If the Soviet Union fighting single-handed not only withstood the onslaught of the German war machine, but also inflicted decisive defeats upon the German fascist troops, all the more hopeless will be the situation of Hitlerite Germany when the main forces of our Allies join in action and the powerful and growing offensive of the armies of all the Allied states develops against Hitlerite Germany.

The German fascist brigands are now tossing about in search of ways to save themselves from disaster. Again they jumped at "total" mobilization in the rear, although Germany's manpower resources are depleted. The fascist ringleaders make desperate attempts to provoke discord in the camp of the anti-Hitler coalition and thereby to drag out the war. Hitlerite diplomats rush from one neutral country to another, strive to establish contacts with pro-Hitler elements, hinting at the possibility of a separate peace now with our state, now with our Allies.

All these subterfuges of the Hitlerites are doomed to failure, as the anti-Hitler coalition is founded on the vital interests of the Allies, who have set themselves the task of smashing Hitlerite Germany and her associates in Europe. It is this very community of basic interests that results in the consolidation of the fighting alliance of the U.S.S.R., Great Britain, and the United States in the progress of the war. The hour is nearing of final reckoning for all the crimes committed by the Hitlerites on Soviet soil and in the occupied countries of Europe.

The victorious offensive of the Red Army became possible thanks to the new labor exploits of the Soviet people in all branches of our national economy. The working people of the Soviet Union buttressed the summer victories of the Red Army on the fronts with new production victories in the rear. Workers of our industry fulfill before the scheduled time and exceed programs fixed by the state; put into commission new factories, blast furnaces and power stations; restore in the liberated districts at unparalleled speed the industry demolished by the occupationists.

The heroic efforts of the working class further strengthen the military material base of the Red Army and thus hasten the hour of our final victory. Soviet peasantry supplies the state with food for the army and cities, with raw materials for industry and renders self-denying support to the Red Army. Soviet intelligentsia renders direct leading aid to the workers and peasants in developing production and meeting the requirements of the Red Army. The working people of the liberated districts daily extend their assistance to the Red Army—their liberator—and add the production of factories and agriculture undergoing restoration to the general stream of front-bound supplies. There is no doubt but that in the future, too, by its heroic labor and by the exertion of all its efforts, the Soviet people will insure the continuous growth of the productive forces of the country for the earliest and final defeat of the German fascist invaders.

The creation of new army formations in the Union Republics, which has been prepared by the fighting companionship of the peoples of the U.S.S.R. in the Patriotic War and by the entire history of our state, will further strengthen the Red Army and will add new fighting forces to its ranks.

Comrades, Red Army men, Red Navy men, sergeants, officers and generals, comrades men and women guerrillas! In the great war of liberation for the freedom and independence of our motherland you have displayed miracles of heroism. The Red Army has achieved a resolute turn in the course of the war in our favor and now marches confidently toward final victory over the enemy. The enemy suffers one defeat after another.

However, he has not yet been smashed. Seeing approaching doom and the inevitability of retribution for all the monstrous crimes they committeed on our soil, the Hitlerite bandits resist with the fury of doomed men. They hurl into battle their last forces and reserves, cling to every meter of Soviet ground, to every advantageous line. For this very reason, no matter how great our successes, we must, just as before, soberly appraise the enemy's strength, be vigilant not to permit self-conceit, complacency, and heedlessness in our ranks. There has been no instance as yet in the history of wars of the enemy jumping into the abyss of himself. To win a war one must lead the enemy to the abyss and push him into it. Only shattering blows steadily growing in their power can crush the resistance of the enemy and bring us to final victory.

With this end in view it is necessary to continue to perfect the combat training of the men and the military art of the commanders of our army. It is the duty of the Red Army daily to raise its military art to a higher level, incessantly and thoroughly to study the enemy's tactics, skillfully and in time to unriddle his insidious tricks, and oppose our own more perfect tactics to the enemy tactics. It is necessary that the combat experience and achievements of the foremost units and formations of the Red Army become the possession of all our troops, that the entire Red Army, all its men and officers, learn to batter the enemy in accordance with all the rules of modern military science.

Comrades, Red Army men and Red Navy men, sergeants, officers and generals, men and women guerrillas! Greeting and congratulating you upon the twenty-sixth anniversary of the Red Army, I order:

1. All rank and file and sergeants' personnel—infantrymen, mortar gunners, artillerymen, fliers, tankmen, sappers, signalmen, cavalrymen—to continue indefatigably to perfect

their combat skill, to make full use of our splendid fighting equipment, to batter the enemy in the way he is battered by our glorious guardsmen, to carry out precisely the orders of commanders, to strengthen discipline and order, to enhance organization.

2. Officers and generals of all arms—to perfect the art of direction of troops, the tactics of maneuvering, the interaction of all arms in the course of battle, to apply more boldly and widely the experience of the advanced units and formations of Guards in combat practice, to raise to a higher level the quality of the staff work and the work of the army rear establishments, to improve and develop our reconnaissance by every means.

3. The entire Red Army—by a skillful combination of fire and maneuver to break up the enemy's defense in its entire depth, to give the enemy no respite, to suppress in time enemy attempts to stem our offensive by counter-attacks, skillfully to organize the pursuit of the enemy, not to allow him to carry away his equipment, by bold maneuver to envelop the flanks of the enemy's troops, to break through to the enemy rear, to surround the enemy's troops, to split and wipe them out if they refuse to down arms.

4. Men and women guerrillas—to increase assistance to the Red Army, to raid the enemy's headquarters and garrisons, to batter his rear establishments, to disrupt his communications and signal service, to deprive him of the possibility of bringing up his reserves.

5. To mark the great victories won by the armed forces of the Soviet State in the course of the past year, today, February 23, on the day of the twenty-sixth anniversary of the Red Army, at 6 P.M., the valiant troops of the Red Army shall be

saluted in Moscow, Leningrad, Kiev, Dniepropetrovsk, Gomel, and Rostov with twenty gun salvos.

Glory to our victorious Red Army!

Glory to Soviet arms!

Glory to our gallant men and women guerrillas!

Long live our great Soviet motherland!

Long live our Communist Party of the Soviet Union—inspirer and organizer of the great victories of the Red Army!

Death to the German invaders!

Order of the Day, February 23, 1944

MAY DAY, 1944

COMRADES, Red Army and Red Navy men, sergeants, officers and generals, men and women guerrillas! Working people of the Soviet Union! Brothers and sisters who have temporarily fallen under the yoke of the German oppressors and have been forcibly driven to fascist penal servitude in Germany:

On behalf of the Soviet Government and of our Bolshevik Party, I greet and congratulate you on May Day!

The peoples of our country meet the day of May First in the midst of outstanding successes of the Red Army. Since the defeat of the German divisions at Stalingrad the Red Army has been conducting a practically incessant offensive. During this time the Red Army has made a fighting advance from the Volga to the Seret, from the foothills of the Caucasus to the Carpathians, exterminating the enemy vermin and sweeping it out of the Soviet land.

In the course of the winter campaign of 1943-44 the Red Army won the historic battle for the Dnieper and for the territories of the Ukraine west of the Dnieper, crushed the powerful German fortified defenses at Leningrad and in the Crimea, by skillful and vigorous actions overwhelmed the German defense on the water barriers of the Yuzhny Bug, the Dniester, the Prut and the Seret. Nearly the entire Ukraine, Moldavia, the Crimea, the Leningrad and Kalinin

Regions, and a considerable part of Byelorussia have been cleared of the German invaders.

The metallurgy of the south, the ore of Krivoi Rog, Kerch and Nikopol, the fertile lands between the Dnieper and the Prut, have been restored to the motherland. Tens of millions of Soviet people have been liberated from fascist slavery.

Acting in the great cause of the liberation of the native land from the fascist invaders, the Red Army emerged on our state frontiers with Rumania and Czechoslovakia and now continues battering the enemy troops on the territory of Rumania.

The successes of the Red Army became possible due to the correct strategy and tactics of the Soviet command, due to the high morale and offensive ardor of our men and commanders, due to our troops being well supplied with first-rate Soviet war equipment, due to the improved skill and training of our artillerymen, mortar gunners, tankmen, fliers, signalmen, sappers, infantrymen, cavalrymen, and scouts.

A considerable contribution to these successes has been made by our great Allies, the United States of America and Great Britain, which hold a front in Italy against the Germans and divert a considerable part of the German troops from us, supply us with very valuable strategical raw materials and armaments, subject to systematic bombardments military objectives in Germany, and thus undermine the latter's military might.

The successes of the Red Army could, however, have proved unstable and could be reduced to nought after the very first serious counter-blow on the part of the enemy were not the Red Army backed from the rear by our entire Soviet people, by our entire country. In the battles for the motherland the Red Army has displayed unexampled heroism. But the

Soviet people has not remained in debt to the Red Army.

Under difficult wartime conditions the Soviet people attained decisive successes in the mass production of armaments, ammunition, clothing and provisions and in their daily delivery to the fronts of the Red Army. During the past year the power of Soviet industry has substantially risen. Hundreds of new factories and mines, and dozens of power-stations, railway lines and bridges have been commissioned.

Fresh millions of Soviet people took their places at machines, mastered the most complex professions, became experts in their jobs. Our collective farms and State farms have stood the trials of war with credit. Under difficult wartime conditions, Soviet peasants work in the fields without folding their hands, supplying our army and population with food and our industry with raw materials.

And our intelligentsia has enriched Soviet science and technology, culture and art, with new outstanding achievements and discoveries. Invaluable services in the cause of the defense of the motherland have been rendered by Soviet women, who work self-sacrificingly in the interests of the front, courageously bear all wartime hardships and inspire to fighting exploits the soldiers of the Red Army—the liberators of our motherland.

The Patriotic War has shown that the Soviet people is capable of performing miracles and emerging victorious from the hardest trials. Workers, collective farmers, intelligentsia, the whole Soviet people, are filled with determination to hasten the defeat of the enemy, to restore completely the economy ruined by the fascists, to make our country still stronger and more prosperous.

Under the blows of the Red Army the bloc of fascist states

is cracking and falling to pieces. Fear and confusion now reign among Hitler's Rumanian, Hungarian, Finnish, and Bulgarian "allies." At present these Hitler underlings, whose countries have been occupied or are being occupied by the Germans, cannot fail to see that Germany has lost the war, Rumania, Hungary, Finland, and Bulgaria have only one possibility for escaping disaster: to break with the Germans and to withdraw from the war.

However, it is difficult to expect that the present governments of these countries will prove capable of breaking with the Germans. One should think that the peoples of these countries will have to take the cause of their liberation from the German yoke into their own hands. And the sooner the peoples of these countries realize to what an impasse the Hitlerites have brought them, the sooner they withdraw all support from their German enslavers and their underlings, the quislings in their own countries, the smaller will be the amount of sacrifices and destruction caused to these countries by the war, the more they can count upon understanding on the part of the democratic countries.

As a result of the successful offensive, the Red Army has emerged on our state frontiers on a stretch of over four hundred kilometers and liberated more than three-quarters of occupied Soviet land from the German fascist yoke. The object now is to clear the whole of our land of the fascist invaders and to re-establish the State frontiers of the Soviet Union along the entire line from the Black Sea to the Barents Sea.

But our tasks cannot be confined to the expulsion of enemy troops from our motherland. The German troops now resemble a wounded beast which is compelled to crawl back to the frontiers of its lair—Germany—in order to heal its wounds. But a wounded beast which has retired to its lair does not cease to be a dangerous beast. To rid our country and the countries allied with us from the danger of enslavement, the wounded beast must be pursued close on its heels and finished off in its own lair. And while pursuing the enemy we must deliver from German bondage our brothers, the Poles and Czechoslovaks, and others allied with us, the peoples of Western Europe, who are under the heel of Hitlerite Germany.

Obviously this task is more difficult than the expulsion of German troops from the Soviet Union. It can be accomplished only on the basis of the joint efforts of the Soviet Union, Great Britain, and the United States of North America, by joint blows from the east dealt by our troops and from the west dealt by the troops of our Allies. There can be no doubt that only such a combined blow can crush completely Hitlerite Germany.

Comrades, Red Army men and Red Navy men, sergeants, officers and generals, men and women guerrillas! Working people of the Soviet Union! Brothers and sisters who have temporarily fallen under the yoke of the German oppressors and have been forcibly driven to fascist penal servitude in Germany! I greet and congratulate you upon the festival of May First!

I order: In honor of the historic victories of the Red Army on the front and to mark the great achievements of the workers, collective farmers, and intelligentsia of the Soviet Union in the rear, today, on the day of the world festival of working people, at 8:00 P.M., a salute of twenty gun salvos shall be fired in Moscow, Leningrad, Gomel, Kiev, Kharkov, Rostov, Tbilisi, Simferopol, and Odessa.

Long live our Soviet motherland!
Long live our Red Army and Navy!
Long live the great Soviet people!
Long live the friendship of the peoples of the Soviet Union!
Long live the Soviet men and women guerrillas!
Eternal glory to the heroes who fell in the battles for the freedom and independence of our motherland!
Death to the German invaders!

Order of the Day, May 1, 1944

THE TWENTY-SEVENTH ANNIVERSARY

OF THE OCTOBER REVOLUTION

COMRADES! Today the Soviet people celebrate the twenty-seventh anniversary of the triumph of the Soviet Revolution in our country. This is the fourth time that our country is observing the anniversary of the Soviet Revolution in the midst of the Patriotic War against the German fascist invaders.

That does not mean, of course, that the fourth year of the war does not differ from the preceding three years of the war in its results. On the contrary, there is a radical difference between them.

Whereas the preceding two years of the war were years when the German forces were on the offensive and when they advanced into the interior of our country—years when the Red Army was compelled to fight defensive actions—and whereas the third year of the war was a year of radical change on our front, when the Red Army launched powerful offensive actions, smashed the Germans in a number of decisive battles, cleared the German troops out of two-thirds of the Soviet territory and compelled them to pass to the defensive while the Red Army was still waging war on the German forces singlehanded without substantial support from the Allies—the fourth year of the war has been a year of decisive victories over the German forces for the Soviet armies and the armies of our Allies, a year in which the Germans, now compelled to fight on two fronts, found themselves flung back to the German frontiers.

In the upshot, this year has ended in the expulsion of the German forces from the Soviet Union, France, Belgium, and central Italy, and the transfer of hostilities to German territory.

The decisive successes of the Red Army this year and the expulsion of the Germans from Soviet territory were predetermined by the succession of shattering blows which our troops dealt the German forces beginning as far back as last January and following then throughout the year under review.

The first blow was struck by our troops in January of this year at Leningrad and Novgorod when the Red Army broke up permanent German defenses and flung the enemy back to the Baltics. This blow resulted in the liberation of the Leningrad Region.

The second blow was struck in February and March of this year on the Bug River when the Red Army routed the German forces and flung them beyond the Dniester. As a result of this blow the Ukraine west of the Dnieper was freed of the German fascist invaders.

The third blow was struck in April and May of this year in the area of the Crimea when the German troops were flung into the Black Sea. As the result of this blow, the Crimea and Odessa were delivered from German oppression.

The fourth blow was struck in June of this year in the area of Karelia, when the Red Army routed the Finnish forces, liberated Vyborg and Petrozavodsk and flung the Finns back into the interior of Finland. This blow resulted in the liberation of the greater part of the Karelo-Finnish Soviet Republic.

The fifth blow was struck at the Germans in June and

July of this year when the Red Army utterly routed the German forces at Vitebsk, Bobruisk, and Mogilev; this blow culminated in the encirclement of thirty German divisions at Minsk. As a result of this blow, our forces: (a) liberated the whole of the Byelorussian Soviet Republic, (b) gained the Vistula and liberated a considerable part of Poland, our ally, (c) gained the Niemen and liberated the greater part of the Lithuanian Soviet Republic, and (d) forced the Niemen and approached the frontiers of Germany.

The sixth blow was struck in July and August of this year in the area of the Western Ukraine when the Red Army routed the German forces at Lvov and flung them beyond the San and the Vistula. As a result of this blow: (a) the Western Ukraine was liberated, and (b) our troops forced the Vistula and set up a strong bridgehead beyond it, west of Sandomir.

The seventh blow was struck in August of this year in the Kishinev and Jassy area when our troops utterly routed the German and Rumanian forces. It culminated in the encirclement of twenty-two German divisions at Kishinev, this number not including Rumanian divisions. As a result of this blow: (a) the Moldavian Soviet Republic was liberated, (b) Germany's Rumanian ally was put out of action and declared war on Germany and Hungary, (c) Germany's Bulgarian ally was put out of action and likewise declared war on Germany, (d) the road was opened for our troops to Hungary, Germany's last ally in Europe, and (e) the opportunity arose to reach out a helping hand to Yugoslavia, our ally, against the German invaders.

The eighth blow was struck in September and October of this year in the Baltics, when the Red Army routed the German forces at Tallinn and Riga and drove them from the Baltics. As a result of this blow: (a) the Estonian Soviet Republic was liberated, (b) the greater part of the Latvian Soviet Republic was liberated, (c) Germany's Finnish ally was put out of action and declared war on Germany, and (d) over thirty German divisions found themselves cut off from Prussia and gripped in pincers between Tukums and Libava where they are now being hammered to a finish by our troops.

In October of this year the ninth blow was launched by our troops between the Tisza and the Danube in the area of Hungary; its purpose is to put Hungary out of the war and turn her against Germany. As a result of this blow which has not yet been consummated: (a) our forces rendered direct assistance to our ally, Yugoslavia, in driving out the Germans and liberating Belgrade, and (b) our forces received the opportunity to cross the Carpathians and reach out a helping hand to our ally, the Czechoslovak Republic, part of whose territory has already been freed of the German fascist invaders.

Lastly, at the end of October of this year, a blow was dealt the German forces in north Finland when the German troops were knocked out of the area of Pechenga and our troops pursuing the Germans entered the territory of Norway, our ally.

I shall not give figures of the losses in killed and prisoners which the enemy sustained in these operations, of the number of guns, tanks, aircraft, shells, and machine guns captured by our troops, and so forth. You are probably acquainted with these figures from the communiques of the Soviet Information Bureau.

Such are the principal operations carried out by the Red Army during the past year, operations which have led to the expulsion of the German forces from our country.

As a result of these operations as many as 120 divisions of the Germans and their allies have been routed and put out of action. In place of the 257 divisions that faced our front last year, of which 207 were German, we now have facing our front, after all the "total" and "super-total" mobilizations, only 204 German and Hungarian divisions, the German divisions numbering no more than 180.

It has to be admitted that in this war Hitler Germany with her fascist army has proved to be a more powerful, crafty and experienced adversary than Germany and her army were in any war of the past. It should be added that in this war the Germans succeeded in exploiting the productive forces of practically the whole of Europe and the quite considerable armies of their vassal states.

And if in spite of these favorable conditions for the prosecution of the war Germany nevertheless finds herself on the brink of imminent destruction, the explanation is that her chief adversary, the Soviet Union, has surpassed Hitler Germany in strength.

What must be regarded as a new factor in the war against Hitler Germany this past year is that this year the Red Army has not been operating against the German forces single-handed as was the case in previous years, but together with the forces of our Allies.

The Teheran Conference was not held for nothing. The decision of the Teheran Conference on a joint blow at Germany from the west, east, and south began to be carried out with amazing precision. Simultaneously with the summer operations of the Red Army on the Soviet-German front, the Allied forces launched the invasion of France and organized powerful offensive operations which compelled Hitler Germany to wage war on two fronts.

The troops and navy of our Allies accomplished a mass landing operation on the coast of France that has no parallel in history for scope and organization, and overcame the German fortifications with consummate skill. Thus Germany found herself gripped in a vise between two fronts.

As was to be expected, the enemy failed to withstand the joint blows of the Red Army and the Allied forces. The enemy's resistance was broken and his troops were knocked out of central Italy, France, Belgium, and the Soviet Union in a short space of time. The enemy was flung back to the German frontier.

There can be no doubt that without the opening of the second front in Europe, which holds as many as 75 German divisions, our troops would not have been able to break the resistance of the German forces and knock them out of the Soviet Union in such a short time.

But it is equally indubitable that without the powerful offensive operations of the Red Army in the summer of this year, which held as many as 200 German divisions, the forces of our Allies could not have coped so quickly with the German forces and knocked them out of central Italy, France, and Belgium. The thing is to keep Germany gripped in this vise between the two fronts. That is the key to victory.

If the Red Army was able to acquit itself successfully of its duty to its country and to drive the Germans from Soviet soil, it was because of the unreserved support received in the rear from our whole country, from all the peoples of our country.

Everything for the front! has been the watchword this past year in the selfless effort of all Soviet people—workers, peasants and intelligentsia, as well as in the directing activities of our government and party bodies.

The past year has been marked by fresh successes in industry, agriculture, and transport, by further progress in our war economy. With the war in its fourth year our factories are producing several times more tanks, aircraft, guns, mortars, and ammunition than in its opening phase.

In the rehabilitation of agriculture the most difficult period has been passed. With the fertile fields of the Don and the Kuban restored to our country and the Ukraine liberated, our farming is recovering rapidly from its grave losses. The Soviet railways have stood a strain that the transport of other countries would hardly be able to bear.

All this indicates that the economic foundation of the Soviet State proved it possessed infinitely greater vitality than the economy of the enemy states. The socialist system born of the October Revolution has lent our people and our army great and invincible strength. Despite the heavy burden of this war, despite the temporary occupation by the Germans of very large and economically important parts of the country, the Soviet State did not reduce the supply of arms and ammunition for the front as the war proceeded, but increased it from year to year. Today the Red Army has not less but more tanks, guns, and aircraft than the German army. As for the quality of our war material, it is far superior to the enemy armaments in that respect.

Just as the Red Army achieved military victory over the fascist forces in its long and arduous single-handed struggle, so the workers in the Soviet rear won economic victory over the enemy in their lone fight against Hitler Germany and her associates.

The Soviet people have denied themselves many necessities, have consciously incurred serious material privations, in order to give more for the front. The unparalleled hardships of the present war have not broken but further tempered the iron will and fearless spirit of the Soviet people. Our people have rightfully won the fame of a heroic nation. Our working class is giving all its strength to the cause of victory, constantly improving the technology of production, increasing the capacity of industrial enterprises, building new factories and mills. The working class of the Soviet Union has a great labor exploit to its credit in the present war.

Our intelligentsia is striking out boldly in the field of technical and cultural innovation, successfully promoting modern science and displaying the creative spirit in applying its achievements to the production of munitions for the Red Army. By their creative work the Soviet intelligentsia has made an invaluable contribution to the enemy's defeat.

An army cannot fight and win without modern armaments. But neither can it fight and win without bread, without provisions. Thanks to the solicitude of the collective farm peasantry, the Red Army experiences no shortage of food in this fourth year of war. The men and women of the collective farms are supplying the workers and intelligentsia with foodstuffs and industry with raw materials, making it possible for factories and mills producing arms and equipment for the front to function normally. Actively and with a clear sense of duty to the country our collective farm peasantry are helping the Red Army to achieve victory over the enemy.

The matchless labor exploits of the Soviet women and of

134

our splendid youth will go down forever in history; for it is they that have borne the brunt of the work in the factories and mills and on the collective and state farms. For the sake of their country's honor and independence Soviet women, youths and girls are displaying true valor and heroism on the labor front. They have shown themselves worthy of their fathers and sons, husbands and brothers, who are defending their homeland against the German fascist fiends.

The labor exploits of the Soviet people in the rear, like the immortal deeds of valor of our soldiers at the front, are rooted in their fervent and life-giving spirit of Soviet patriotism. The strength of Soviet patriotism lies in the fact that it is based not on racial or nationalistic prejudices, but on the people's profound devotion and loyalty to their Soviet homeland, on the fraternal partnership of the working people of all the nationalities in our land.

Soviet patriotism blends harmoniously the national traditions of the peoples and the common vital interests of all the working peoples of the Soviet Union. Far from dividing them, Soviet patriotism welds all the nations and peoples of our country into a single fraternal family. This should be regarded as the foundation of the inviolable and ever stronger friendship among the peoples of the Soviet Union.

At the same time the peoples of the U.S.S.R. respect the rights and independence of the nations of foreign countries and have always shown themselves willing to live in peace and friendship with their neighbor states. This should be regarded as the foundation of the contacts growing and gaining strength between our state and the freedom-loving nations. The reason Soviet men and women hate the German invaders is not that they are of different nationality, but that they have brought untold calamity and suffering on our people and on all freedom-loving nations. It is an old saying of our people that the wolf is not beaten for being gray but for devouring sheep.

The German fascists chose the misanthropic race theory for their ideological weapon in the expectation that by preaching bestial nationalism they would produce the moral and political conditions for the German invaders' domination over the subjugated nations. Actually, however, the policy of racial hatred pursued by the Hitlerites has proved a source of weakness for the German fascist state internally and of its isolation internationally.

The ideology and policy of racial hatred have been a factor in the disintegration of Hitler's brigand bloc. It cannot be regarded as an accident that not only the subjugated peoples of France and Yugoslavia, Poland and Czechoslovakia, Greece and Belgium, Denmark, Norway, and the Netherlands have risen against the German imperialists, but also Hitler's former vassals—the Italians and Rumanians, Finns, and Bulgarians. By their savage policy the Hitler clique have set all the nations of the world against Germany, and the so-called "chosen German race" has become the object of universal hatred.

It is not only military defeat that the Hitlerites have sustained in this war, but moral and political defeat as well. The ideology of equality of all races and nations which has taken firm root in our country, the ideology of friendship among the peoples, has emerged completely victorious over the Hitlerite ideology of bestial nationalism and racial hatred.

Today when the Patriotic War is drawing to its victorious conclusion, the historic role of the Soviet people is revealed in its full greatness. It is universally acknowledged now that by their selfless struggle the Soviet people have saved the civilization of Europe from the fascist vandals. That is the great service rendered by the Soviet people to the history of mankind.

The past year has been a year of triumph for the common cause of the anti-German coalition, for the sake of which the peoples of the Soviet Union, Great Britain and the United States have joined in a fighting alliance. It has been a year of consolidation of the unity of the three main powers and of co-ordination of their actions against Hitler Germany.

The Teheran Conference decision on joint actions against Germany and the brilliant realization of that decision is one of the striking indications of the consolidation of the anti-Hitlerite coalition front. There are few instances in history of plans for large-scale military operations undertaken in joint actions against a common enemy being carried out so fully and with such precision as the plan for a joint blow against Germany drawn up at the Teheran Conference. There can be no doubt that without unity of opinion and co-ordination of actions between the three great powers, the Teheran decision could not have been put into effect so fully and with such precision. Nor, on the other hand, can there be any doubt that the successful realization of the Teheran decision was bound to serve for the consolidation of the United Nations front.

An equally striking indication of the solidity of the front of the United Nations is to be seen in the decisions of the Dumbarton Oaks Conference on post-war security. There is talk of differences between the three powers on certain security problems. Differences do exist, of course, and they will arise on a number of other issues as well. Differences of opinion

137

are to be found even among people in one and the same party. They are all the more bound to occur between representatives of different states and different parties.

The surprising thing is not that differences exist, but that there are so few of them and that as a rule in practically every case they are resolved in a spirit of unity and co-ordination among the three great powers.

What matters is not that there are differences, but that these differences do not transgress the bounds of what the interests of unity of the three great powers allow, and that in the long run they are resolved in accordance with the interests of that unity. It is known that more serious differences existed between us over the opening of the second front. It is also known, however, that in the end these differences were resolved in a spirit of complete accord.

The same thing may be said of the differences at the Dumbarton Oaks Conference. What is characteristic about this conference is not that certain differences were revealed there, but that nine-tenths of the security problems were dispatched at this conference in a spirit of complete unanimity. That is why I think that the Dumbarton Oaks Conference decisions are to be regarded as a striking indication of the solidity of the front of the anti-German coalition.

The recent talks in Moscow with Mr. Churchill, the head of the British government, and Mr. Eden, the British Foreign Secretary, are to be viewed as an even more striking indication of the consolidation of the United Nations front, held as these talks were in an atmosphere of friendship and a spirit of perfect unanimity. All through the war the Hitlerites have been making frantic efforts to cause disunion among the United Nations and set them at loggerheads, to stir up suspicion and unfriendly feeling among them, to weaken their war effort by mutual mistrust and if possible by conflict between them as well.

Ambitions like these on the part of the Hitler politicians are easy enough to understand. There is no greater danger for them than the unity of the United Nations in the struggle against Hitler imperialism, and they could achieve no greater military-political success than by dividing the Allied powers in their fight against the common foe.

It is well known, however, how futile the efforts of the fascist politicians to disrupt the alliance of the great powers have proved. That means that the alliance between the U.S.S.R., Great Britain, and the United States is founded not on casual, short-lived considerations but on vital and lasting interests. There need be no doubt that having stood the strain of over three years of war and being sealed with the blood of nations risen in defense of their liberty and honor, the fighting alliance of the democratic powers will all the more certainly stand the strain of the concluding phase of the war.

However, the past year has been not only a year of the consolidation of the anti-German front of the Allied powers, but also a year of its extension. It cannot be regarded as an accident that after Italy, other allies of Germany—Finland, Rumania and Bulgaria—have also been put out of the war. A point to be made is that these states have not only withdrawn from the war but have broken with Germany and declared war on her, thus joining the front of the United Nations. That is certainly an extension of the United Nations front against Hitler Germany.

Without doubt Germany's last ally in Europe, Hungary,

will also be put out of action in the nearest future. This will mean the complete isolation of Hitler Germany in Europe and the inevitability of her collapse.

The United Nations face the victorious conclusion of the war against Hitler Germany. The war against Germany will be won by the United Nations—of that there can no longer be any doubt today.

To win the war against Germany is to accomplish a great historical task. But winning the war is not in itself synonymous with insuring for the nations lasting peace and guaranteed security in the future. The thing is not only to win the war but also to render new aggression and new war impossible, if not forever then at least for a long time to come.

After her defeat Germany will of course be disarmed both in the economic and the military-political sense. It would however be naïve to think that she will not attempt to restore her might and launch new aggression. It is common knowledge that the German chieftains are already now preparing for a new war. History reveals that a short period of time, some twenty or thirty years, is enough for Germany to recover from defeat and re-establish her might.

What means are there to preclude fresh aggression on Germany's part, and, if war should start nevertheless, to nip it in the bud and allow it no opportunity to develop into a big war?

The question is the more in place since history shows that aggressive nations, as the nations that attack, are usually better prepared for a new war than peace-loving nations which, having no interest in a new war, are usually behind with their preparations for it. It is a fact that in the present war the aggressive nations had an invasion army all ready even before the war broke out; while the peace-loving nations did not have even a fully adequate army to cover the mobilization.

One cannot regard as an accident such distasteful facts as the Pearl Harbor "incident," the loss of the Philippines and other Pacific islands, the loss of Hongkong and Singapore, when Japan as the aggressor nation proved to be better prepared for war than Great Britain and the United States of America, which pursued a policy of peace. Nor can one regard as an accident such a distasteful fact as the loss of the Ukraine, Byelorussia, and the Baltics in the very first year of the war, when Germany as the aggressive nation proved better prepared for war than the peace-loving Soviet Union.

It would be naïve to explain these facts by the personal qualities of the Japanese and the Germans, their superiority over the British, the Americans, and the Russians, their foresight and so on. The reason here is not personal qualities but the fact that the aggressive nations interested in a new war, being nations that prepare for war over a long time and accumulate forces for it, are usually—and are bound to be— better prepared for war than peace-loving nations which have no interest in a new war. That is natural and understandable. If you like, this is a law of history which it would be dangerous to ignore.

It is not to be denied accordingly that in days to come the peace-loving nations may once more find themselves caught off their guard by aggression, unless of course they work out special measures right now which can avert it.

Well, what means are there to preclude fresh aggression on Germany's part, and, if war should start nevertheless, to nip it in the bud and give it no opportunity to develop into a big war?

There is only one means to this end, in addition to the complete disarmament of the aggressive nations: that is, to establish a special organization made up of representatives of the peace-loving nations to uphold peace and safeguard security; to put the necessary minimum of armed forces required for the averting of aggression at the disposal of the directing body of this organization, and to obligate this organization to employ these armed forces without delay if it becomes necessary to avert or stop aggression and punish the culprits.

This must not be a repetition of the ill-starred League of Nations which had neither the right nor the means to avert aggression. It will be a new, special, fully authorized world organization having at its command everything necessary to uphold peace and avert new aggression.

Can we expect the actions of this world organization to be sufficiently effective? They will be effective if the great powers which have borne the brunt of the war against Hitler Germany continue to act in a spirit of unanimity and accord. They will not be effective if this essential condition is violated.

Comrades, the Soviet people and the Red Army are performing successfully the tasks that have confronted them in the course of the Patriotic War. The Red Army has done its patriotic duty with credit and has freed our country of the enemy. Now and for all time our land is clear of the Hitlerite pollution. For the Red Army there now remains its last final mission: together with the armies of our Allies to consummate the defeat of the German fascist army, to finish off the fascist beast in his own den and hoist the flag of victory over Berlin. There is reason to expect that this task will be performed by the Red Army in the none too distant future.

Long live our victorious Red Army!
Long live our glorious Navy!
Long live the mighty Soviet people!
Long live our great homeland!
Death to the German-fascist invaders!

Speech delivered at Moscow, November 6, 1944

THE TWENTY-SEVENTH ANNIVERSARY

OF THE OCTOBER REVOLUTION

COMRADES, Red Army men and Red Navy men, sergeants, officers and generals! Working people of the Soviet Union! Brothers and sisters forcibly driven to fascist convict labor in Germany:

On behalf of the Soviet Government and our Bolshevik Party I greet and congratulate you upon the twenty-seventh anniversary of the great October Socialist Revolution. We celebrate the twenty-seventh anniversary of the October Revolution in the midst of decisive victories of the Red Army over the enemies of our homeland.

By the heroic efforts of the Red Army and the Soviet people our land has been cleared of the German fascist invaders. This year Soviet troops incessantly rained blows on the enemy, one stronger than the other.

In the winter of 1943 the Red Army scored outstanding victories in the Ukraine, west of the Dnieper, and routed the Germans at Leningrad. In the spring of this year the Red Army cleared the Crimea of Germans. In the summer of 1944 our troops inflicted major defeats upon the Hitlerite army, which had as their result a radical change of the situation on the front of struggle with the German fascist invaders.

The Red Army crushed the enemy's powerful defense in the Karelian Isthmus, also between Ladoga and Onega Lakes, and knocked Finland out of the Hitlerite brigand bloc.

In the historical battle on the Byelorussian lands, Red Army

144

troops utterly routed the central group of German troops, which consisted of three armies, and annihilated or took prisoner 540,000 German officers and men.

In the battle in the south the Red Army surrounded and completely annihilated the group of German troops, which consisted of two armies. In this the Soviet troops wiped out or took prisoner over 250,000 German officers and men.

The Red Army smashed the Germans in Rumania, threw them out of Bulgaria, is battering the Germans on the territory of Hungary. Our troops crushed the Baltic group of the Hitlerite army. During the summer campaign of 1944, the Red Army fought its way from Kishinev to Belgrade—over 900 kilometers; from Zhlobin to Warsaw—over 600 kilometers; from Vitebsk to Tilsit—550 kilometers. The war has been carried now to the territory of fascist Germany.

In the course of the fighting the Red Army ejected the German fascist invaders from the entire territory of the Soviet Ukraine and Byelorussia, the Karelo-Finnish, Moldavian, Estonian, Latvian, and Lithuanian Soviet Republics.

The fascist yoke of three years on the lands of our fraternal Soviet Republics temporarily seized by the Germans has been overthrown. The Red Army restored freedom to tens of millions of Soviet people.

The Soviet state boundary treacherously violated by the Hitlerite hordes on June 22, 1941, has been re-established throughout its length from the Black to the Barents Seas.

The past year thus has been a year of the complete liberation of the Soviet land from the German fascist invaders. After completing the liberation of its native land from the Hitlerite pollution the Red Army is now helping the peoples of Poland, Yugoslavia and Czechoslovakia to break the chains of fascist slavery and regain their freedom and independence.

In the winter and summer battles of the past year the Red Army demonstrated its grown military mastery. Red Army soldiers skillfully smashed the enemy's fortified zones, vigorously pursued, encircled and wiped out the enemy.

Efficient co-ordination of all Soviet arms and high skill in maneuvering have been demonstrated in offensive battles. Soviet soldiers grew steeled in battles, learned to batter and vanquish the enemy. The Red Army has grown into a redoubtable force and is superior to the enemy in military skill and fighting equipment.

The Red Army's forces are multiplied many times over by the efficient work of the Soviet rear. Workers, collective farmers, and intellectuals fulfill their duty to the motherland with credit, heroically overcome wartime difficulties, uninterruptedly supply the Red Army with armaments, ammunition and provisions. The Soviet economy continuously increases its strength and renders ever-growing assistance to the front.

The Red Army and the Soviet people are ready to strike fresh crushing blows at the enemy. The days of the Hitlerite sanguinary regime are numbered. Under the blows of the Red Army the fascist bloc has finally crumbled to pieces; Hitlerite Germany has lost most of her allies.

The large-scale operations carried out with consummate skill by the armies of our Allies in Western Europe resulted in the debacle of the German troops in France and Belgium, and the liberation of these countries from fascist occupation.

The Allied troops crossed Germany's western frontier. The joint blows dealt by the Red Army and the Anglo-American troops to Hitlerite Germany brought nearer the hour of the victorious termination of the war. The ring around Hitlerite

Germany is closing. The den of the fascist beast has been invested on all sides, and no artifices of the enemy will save him from imminent complete defeat.

The Red Army and the armies of our Allies have taken up initial positions for the decisive offensive on Germany's vital centers. The task now is to crush Hitlerite Germany within the shortest time by the vigorous onslaught of the armies of the United Nations.

Comrades, Red Army men and Red Navy men, sergeants, officers, and generals! Working people of the Soviet Union!

In the great Patriotic War we defended our motherland from the invaders, finally eliminated the threat of enslavement of the peoples of the U.S.S.R. by the fascist fiends, and now stand on the threshold of complete victory.

To mark the historic victories of the Red Army at the front and the great achievements of the workers, peasants, and intellectuals in the rear, in honor of the liberation of the Soviet land from the German fascist invaders, I order:

Today, on the day of the twenty-seventh anniversary of the great October Socialist Revolution, at 8 P.M., a salute of twenty-four gun salvos be fired in Moscow, Leningrad, Kiev, Minsk, Petrozavodsk, Tallinn, Riga, Vilnius, Kishinev, Tbilisi, Sevastopol, Lvov.

Hail the twenty-seventh anniversary of the great October Socialist Revolution!

Long live our free Soviet country! Long live our Red Army and Navy! Long live the great Soviet people!

Eternal glory to the heroes who fell in the struggle for the freedom and independence of our motherland!

Order of the Day, November 7, 1944

147

THE TWENTY-SEVENTH ANNIVERSARY

OF THE FOUNDING OF THE RED

ARMY

COMRADES, Red Army men and Red Navy men, sergeants, officers and generals!

Today we are celebrating the twenty-seventh anniversary of the Red Army's existence. Created by the great Lenin to defend our motherland from attack of foreign invaders and reared by the Bolshevik Party, the Red Army traversed a glorious path in its development.

It has fulfilled with credit its historical destination and rightfully is the beloved child of the Soviet people. In the years of civil war, the Red Army defended the young Soviet state from numerous enemies. In the great battles of the patriotic war against the German invasion, the Red Army saved the peoples of the Soviet Union from German fascist slavery and upheld the freedom and independence of our motherland, and helped the peoples of Europe to cast off the German yoke.

Now we are celebrating the twenty-seventh anniversary of the Red Army in the midst of fresh historical victories over the enemy. The Red Army has not only freed its native land of Hitlerite filth but also hurled the enemy for many hundred kilometers back beyond those lines from which the Germans launched their bandit attack upon our country, carried the war into Germany's territory, and now, together with the armies of our allies, is successfully completing the rout of the German fascist army.

In January of this year, the Red Army brought down upon the enemy a blow of unparalleled force along the entire front from the Baltic to the Carpathians. On a stretch of 1,200 kilometers it broke up a powerful defense of the Germans which they had been building for a number of years. In the course of the offensive, the Red Army by its swift and skillful actions has hurled the enemy far back to the west. In stiff fighting, Soviet troops advanced from the frontiers of East Prussia to the lower reaches of the Vistula—for 270 kilometers; from the Vistula bridgehead, south of Warsaw, to the lower reaches of the Oder—for 570 kilometers; from Sandomierz bridgehead into the depth of German Silesia—for 480 kilometers.

The first consequence of the successes of our winter offensive was that they thwarted the Germans' winter offensive in the west, which was aimed at the seizure of Belgium and Alsace, and enabled the armies of our allies in their turn to launch an offensive against the Germans and thus link up their offensive operations in the west with offensive operations of the Red Army in the east.

Within 40 days of the offensive in January-February, 1945, our troops ejected the Germans from 300 towns, captured about 100 war plants, manufacturing tanks, aircraft, armaments and ammunition, occupied over 2,400 railway stations, and seized a network of railways totalling over 15,000 kilometers in length.

Within this short period, Germany lost over 350,000 officers and men in war prisoners and not less than 800,000 in killed.

During the same period, the Red Army destroyed or seized

about 3,000 German aircraft, over 4,500 tanks and self-propelled guns and not less than 12,000 guns.

As a result, the Red Army completely liberated Poland and a considerable part of the territory of Czechoslovakia, occupied Budapest and put out of the war Germany's last ally in Europe —Hungary—captured the greater part of East Prussia and German Silesia and battled its way into Brandenburg, into Pomerania, to the approaches of Berlin.

The Hitlerites boasted that for more than one hundred years no single enemy soldier was within Germany's borders and that the German army fought and would fight only on foreign soil. Now an end has been put to this German braggery. Our winter offensive has shown that the Red Army finds more and more strength for the solution of ever more complex and difficult problems.

Its glorious soldiers have learned to batter and annihilate the enemy in accordance with all rules of modern military science. Our soldiers, inspired by the realization of their great mission of liberation, display miraculous heroism and selflessness; all combine gallantry and audacity in battle with the full utilization of the power and might of their weapons.

The Red Army generals and officers masterfully combine massed blows of powerful equipment with skillful and swift maneuver. In the fourth year of war, the Red Army has grown stronger and mightier than ever before, its combat equipment has become more perfect and its fighting mastership many times higher.

Comrades, Red Army men, Red Navy men, sergeants, officers and generals: Complete victory over the Germans is now already near. But victory never comes of itself—it is won in hard battles and in persistent labor.

The doomed enemy hurls his last forces into action, resists desperately in order to escape stern retribution. He grasps and will grasp at the most extreme and base means of struggle. Therefore, it should be borne in mind that the nearer our victory, the higher must be our vigilance, the heavier must be our blows at the enemy.

On behalf of the Soviet government and our glorious Bolshevik Party, I greet and congratulate you upon the twenty-seventh anniversary of the Red Army!

To mark the great victories achieved by the armed forces of the Soviet state in the course of the past year, I order:

Today, Feb. 23, on the day of the twenty-seventh anniversary of the Red Army, at 8 p.m., a salute of 20 artillery salvoes shall be fired in Moscow, Leningrad, Kiev, Minsk, Petrozavodsk, Tallinn, Riga, Vilnius, Kishinev, Tbilisi, Stalingrad Sevastopol, Odessa, and Lwow.

Long live our victorious Red Army!

Long live our victorious Navy!

Long live our mighty Soviet motherland!

Eternal glory to the heroes who fell in the struggle for freedom and independence of our motherland!

Death to the German invaders!

Order of the Day, February 23, 1945.

THE SOVIET-POLISH TREATY

M R. PRESIDENT, Mr. Prime Minister, Gentlemen!
I believe that the treaty of friendship, mutual assistance and postwar collaboration between the Soviet
Union and Poland which we have just signed is of great historical importance. The importance of this treaty consists, in
the first place, in that it signifies a radical turn in relations
between the Soviet Union and Poland toward alliance and
friendship, a turn which took shape in the course of the
present liberation struggle against Germany and which is
now being formally consummated in this treaty.

It is well known that the relations between our countries in
the course of the past five centuries were marked by mutual
estrangement, unfriendliness and not infrequently by open
military conflicts. Such relations weakened both our countries
and strengthened German imperialism. The importance of
the present treaty consists in that it puts an end to these old
relations between our countries, nails down the lid of the
coffin over them and creates a real basis for replacing the old
unfriendly relations with relations of alliance and friendship
between the Soviet Union and Poland.

In the course of the past twenty-five to thirty years, that is,
in the course of the last two World Wars, the Germans succeeded in making use of the territory of Poland as a corridor
for an invasion of the East and as a springboard for an attack

on the Soviet Union. This became possible because at that time there were no friendly allied relations between our countries. The former rulers of Poland did not want to have relations of alliance with the Soviet Union. They preferred a policy of playing up Germany against the Soviet Union. And of course they played themselves into trouble. Poland was occupied, her independence abolished, and as a result of this whole ruinous policy, German troops were enabled to appear at the gates of Moscow.

The importance of the present treaty consists in that it puts an end to the old and ruinous policy of playing up Germany against the Soviet Union and replaces it by a policy of alliance and friendship between Poland and her eastern neighbor. Such is the historical importance of the treaty of friendship, mutual assistance, and postwar collaboration between Poland and the Soviet Union which we have just signed.

No wonder, therefore, that the peoples of our countries impatiently await the signing of this treaty. They feel that this treaty is a pledge of the independence of the new democratic Poland, a pledge of her might, her prosperity.

But this is not all. The present treaty has also great international significance. As long as there was no alliance between our countries, Germany was able to take advantage of the absence of a united front between us, she could oppose Poland to the Soviet Union and vice versa, and thus beat them one at a time. This has changed radically with the alliance between our countries. Now it is no longer possible to oppose our countries to each other. Now there is a united front between our countries from the Baltic to the Carpathians against the common enemy, against German imperialism. Now one may confidently say that German aggression is besieged from the East.

Undoubtedly if this barrier in the East is supplemented by a barrier in the West, that is, by an alliance between our countries and our Allies in the West, one may safely say that German aggression will be curbed and it will not be easy for it to run loose.

No wonder, therefore, that the freedom-loving nations and, in the first place, the Slav nations, impatiently await the conclusion of this treaty, for they see that this treaty signifies the strengthening of the united front of the United Nations against the common enemy in Europe. Therefore, I do not doubt that our Allies in the West will welcome this treaty.

May free, independent, democratic Poland live and prosper! May her eastern neighbor, our Soviet Union, live and prosper! Long live the alliance and friendship between our countries!

Speech delivered on the signing of the Soviet-Polish Treaty, Moscow, April 22, 1945

THE MEETING OF THE SOVIET AND

ALLIED ARMIES

THE VICTORIOUS ARMIES of the Allied powers, waging a war of liberation in Europe, have routed the German troops and linked up on the territory of Germany.

Our task and our duty is to finish off the enemy, to compel him to ground arms and surrender unconditionally. The Red Army will fulfill to the end this task and this duty to our people and to all freedom-loving nations.

We hail the gallant troops of our Allies now standing on the territory of Germany, shoulder to shoulder with Soviet troops, and filled with determination to discharge their duty to the end.

Radio Address, Moscow, April 28, 1945

155

MAY DAY, 1945

COMRADES Red Army men and Red Navy men, sergeants and petty officers, officers of the Army and Navy, generals and admirals! Working people of the Soviet Union!

Today our country is celebrating May First—the international holiday of the working people. This year the peoples of our Motherland are celebrating May Day under the conditions of the victorious termination of the Great Patriotic War.

The hard times, when the Red Army fought back the enemy troops at Moscow and Leningrad, at Grozny and Stalingrad, are gone, never to return. Now our victorious troops are battering the enemy's armed forces in the center of Germany, far beyond Berlin, on the Elbe River.

Within a short time Poland, Hungary, the greater part of Czechoslovakia, a considerable part of Austria and her capital, Vienna, have been liberated. At the same time the Red Army has captured East Prussia—spearhead of German imperialism, Pomerania, the greater part of Brandenburg, and the main districts of Germany's capital, Berlin, having hoisted the banner of victory over Berlin.

As a result of these offensive battles fought by the Red Army, within three or four months the Germans lost over 800,000 officers and men in prisoners and about one million killed. During the same period, Red Army troops captured or destroyed about 6,000 enemy airplanes, about 12,000 tanks and self-propelled guns, over 23,000 field guns, and enormous quantities of other armaments and equipment.

It should be noted that in these battles, Polish, Yugoslav, Czechoslovak, Bulgarian and Rumanian divisions successfully advanced against the common enemy side by side with the Red Army.

As a result of the Red Army's shattering blows, the German command was compelled to transfer dozens of divisions to the Soviet-German front, baring whole sectors on the other fronts. This circumstance helped the forces of our Allies to develop a successful offensive in the West.

Thus by simultaneous blows at the German troops from East and West, the troops of the Allies and the Red Army were able to split the German forces into two isolated parts and to effect a junction of our own and the Allied troops in a united front. There can be no doubt that this circumstance means the end of Hitlerite Germany.

The days of Hitlerite Germany are numbered. More than half her territory is occupied by the Red Army and by the troops of our Allies. Germany has lost her most important vital districts. The industry remaining in the Hitlerites' hands cannot supply the German army with sufficient quantities of armaments, ammunition and fuel. The manpower reserves of the German army are depleted. Germany is completely isolated and stands alone, if one does not count her ally—Japan.

In search of a way out of their hopeless plight, the Hitlerite adventurers resort to all kinds of tricks, even going as far as making advances to the Allies in an effort to cause dissension in the Allied camp. These new knavish tricks of the Hitlerites are doomed to utter failure. They can only accelerate the disintegration of the German troops.

The mendacious fascist propaganda intimidates the German population with absurd tales alleging that the Armies of the United Nations wish to exterminate the German people. The United Nations do not set themselves the task of destroying the German people. The United Nations will destroy fascism and German militarism, will severely punish the war criminals, and will compel the Germans to compensate the damage they caused to other countries. But the United Nations do not molest and will not molest Germany's peaceful population if it modestly fulfills the demands of the Allied military authorities.

The brilliant victories won by Soviet troops in the Great Patriotic War have demonstrated the heroic might of the Red Army and its high military skill. In the progress of the war our Motherland has acquired a first-rate regular army, capable of upholding the great socialist achievements of our people and of securing the state interests of the Soviet Union. Despite the fact that the Soviet Union for four years has been waging a war on an unparalleled scale demanding colossal expenditures, our socialist economic system is gaining strength and developing, while the economy of the liberated regions, plundered and ruined by the German invaders, is successfully and swiftly reviving. This is the result of the heroic efforts of the workers and collective farmers, of the Soviet intellectuals, of the women and youth of our country, inspired and guided by the great Bolshevik Party.

The World War unleashed by the German imperialists is drawing to a close. The collapse of Hitlerite Germany is a matter of the immediate future. The Hitlerite ringleaders who imagined themselves the rulers of the world have found themselves ruined. The mortally wounded fascist beast is breathing his last. One thing is now required—to deal the death blow to the fascist beast.

Soldiers of the Red Army and Navy! The last storming of the Hitlerite den is on. Set new examples of military skill and gallantry in the final battles. Smite the enemy more heavily, skilfully break up his defense, pursue and surround the German invaders, give them no respite until they cease resistance. When beyond the border of your native land, be especially vigilant! Uphold the honor and dignity of the Soviet soldier as heretofore!

Working people of the Soviet Union! By persistent and indefatigable work, increase the all-round assistance to the front. Swiftly heal the wounds inflicted on the country by the war, raise still higher the might of our Soviet state!

Comrades, Red Army men and Red Navy men, sergeants and petty officers, officers of the Army and Navy, generals and admirals! Working people of the Soviet Union! On behalf of the Soviet government and of our Bolshevik Party I greet and congratulate you on May first!

In honor of the historic victories of the Red Army at the front and of the great achievements of the workers, collective farmers and intellectuals in the rear, to mark the international holiday of working people, I hereby order:

Today, on May first, a salute of twenty artillery salvos shall be fired in the capitals of the Union Republics: Moscow, Kiev, Minsk, Baku, Tbilisi, Erevan, Ashkhabad, Tashkent, Stalinabad, Alma-Ata, Frunze, Petrozavodsk, Kishinev, Vilnius, Riga and Tallinn, as well as in the hero cities of Leningrad, Stalingrad, Sevastopol and Odessa.

Long live our mighty Soviet Motherland!

Long live the great and victorious Soviet people!

Long live the victorious Red Army and Navy!

Eternal glory to the heroes who fell in the battles for the freedom and independence of our Motherland!

Forward to the final rout of Hitlerite Germany!

Order of the Day, May 1, 1945

VICTORY!

COMRADES, my countrymen and women!
The great day of victory over Germany has come.
Fascist Germany has been brought to her knees by the
Red Army and the troops of our Allies, has acknowledged
herself beaten, and has declared her unconditional surrender.

On May 7 the preliminary act of capitulation was signed in
Reims. On May 8, in the presence of the staff of the Russian
High Command and in the presence of representatives of the
Supreme Command of the Allied Forces, the final act of
capitulation, which came into force at 2400 hours May 8, was
signed in Berlin.

Knowing the wolflike actions of the Germans, who consider
treaties and agreements as so much paper, we have no reason
to believe their word. However, since this morning German
troops, in fulfillment of the act of capitulation, began laying
down their arms and surrendering to our troops.

That is no longer an empty scrap of paper. That is the real
capitulation of Germany's armed forces. It is true, one group of
German troops in the area of Czechoslovakia still avoids capitulation, but I hope the Red Army will succeed in bringing it
to its senses.

We now have all the ground for declaring that the historic
day of the final rout of Germany has come—the day of great
victory of our people over German imperialism.

The great sacrifices that we have made in the name of the
liberty and independence of our Motherland, the innumerable
exertions and sufferings that our people had to bear in the
course of the war, the strenuous work in the rear and the front

that they have brought to the altar of the Fatherland, have not been in vain. They have been crowned by complete victory over the enemy.

The centuries-old struggle of the Slav peoples for their existence and their independence has been concluded by victory over the German invaders and over German tyranny. From now on, over Europe will fly the banner dear to us—the banner of victory of the peoples and of peace among nations.

Three years ago Hitler publicly declared that his plans included carving up the Soviet Union and depriving it of the Caucasus, the Ukraine, White Russia and the Baltic States and other districts. Hitler said openly that "we shall destroy Russia so that she will never be able to rise again."

That was three years ago. But Hitler's insane ideas were not destined to be fulfilled. In the course of the war they were blown into dust. In actual fact, the opposite happened to that which the Hitlerites threatened. Germany is completely destroyed. German troops are capitulating and the Soviet Union triumphs in victory, although it does not intend either to dismember or to annihilate Germany.

Comrades, the Great Patriotic War has ended in our complete victory. The period of war in Europe has ended. The period of peaceful development has begun.

Glory to our heroic Red Army, which has defended the independence of our Motherland and achieved victory over the enemy! Glory to our victorious people!

Eternal glory to the heroes who fell in battle against the enemy and gave their lives for the freedom and happiness of our Motherland!

Radio Speech, Moscow, May 9, 1945

"LONG LIVE THE VICTORIOUS RED

ARMY AND NAVY"

O N MAY 8, 1945, an instrument of the unconditional surrender of the German armed forces was signed in Berlin by representatives of the German High Command.

The Great Patriotic War waged by the Soviet people against the German-fascist invaders has been victoriously completed. Germany has been completely routed.

Comrades, Red Army men, Red Navy men, sergeants, warrant officers, officers of the Army and Navy, generals, admirals, marshals! I congratulate you upon the victorious conclusion of the Great Patriotic War!

To mark the complete victory over Germany, today, May 9, on the day of victory, at ten P.M., the capital of our Motherland, Moscow, on behalf of the Motherland, will salute the gallant troops of the Red Army and the ships and units of the Navy who have achieved this brilliant victory with thirty artillery salvos from one thousand guns.

Eternal glory to the heroes who fell in the battles for the freedom and independence of our Motherland!

Long live the victorious Red Army and Navy!

Order of the Day, May 9, 1945

LETTERS FROM JOSEPH STALIN

I. REPLY TO LETTER FROM HENRY C. CASSIDY, MOSCOW CORRE-
SPONDENT OF THE ASSOCIATED PRESS

Dear Mr. Cassidy:

Owing to the pressure of work and my consequent inability to grant you an interview, I shall confine myself to a brief written answer to your questions.

1. What place does the possibility of a second front occupy in the Soviet estimates of the current situation?

ANSWER: *A most important place; one might say a place of first-rate importance.*

2. To what extent is Allied aid to the Soviet Union proving effective and what could be done to amplify and improve this aid?

ANSWER: *As compared with the aid which the Soviet Union is giving to the Allies by drawing upon itself the main force of the German fascist armies, the aid of the Allies to the Soviet Union has so far been little effective. In order to amplify and improve this aid, only one thing is required: that the Allies fulfill their obligations fully and on time.*

3. What remains of the Soviet capacity for resistance?

ANSWER: *I think that the Soviet capacity of resisting the German brigands is in strength not less, if not greater, than the*

163

*capacity of fascist Germany or of any other aggressive power
to secure for itself world domination.
October 3, 1942*

Dear Mr. Cassidy:

*I am answering your questions which reached me on No-
vember 12.*

*1. What is the Soviet view of the Allied campaign in
Africa?*

ANSWER: *The Soviet view of this campaign is that it repre-
sents an outstanding fact of major importance demonstrating
the growing might of the armed forces of the Allies and opening the prospect of the disintegration of the Italo-German
coalition in the very near future.*

*The campaign in Africa refutes once more the skeptics who
affirm that Anglo-American leaders are not capable of organizing a serious war campaign. There can be no doubt that no
one but first-rate organizers could carry out such serious war
operations as the successful landings in North Africa across
the ocean, as the quick occupation of harbors and wide territories from Casablanca to Bougie, and as the smashing of Italo-
German armies in the western desert being effected with such
mastery.*

*2. How effective has this campaign been in relieving pres-
sure on the Soviet Union, and what further aid does the Soviet
Union await?*

ANSWER: *It is yet too soon to say to what an extent this campaign has been effective in relieving immediate pressure on the*

164

*Soviet Union. But it may be confidently said that the effect will
not be a small one and that a certain relief in pressure on the
Soviet Union will result in the nearest future.*

*But that is not the only thing that matters. What matters
first of all is that since the campaign in Africa means that the
initiative has passed into the hands of our Allies, the campaign
changes radically the political and war situation in Europe in
favor of the Anglo-Soviet-American coalition; that the campaign undermines the prestige of Hitlerite Germany as a leading force in the system of Axis powers and demoralizes Hitler's allies in Europe; the campaign releases France from her
state of lethargy, mobilizes anti-Hitler forces of France and
provides a basis for building up an anti-Hitler French army;
also the campaign creates conditions for putting Italy out of
commission and for isolating Hitlerite Germany; finally,
that the campaign creates the prerequisites for establishment
of a second front in Europe nearer to Germany's vital centers
which will be of decisive importance for organizing victory
over Hitlerite tyranny.*

*3. What possibility is there of Soviet offensive power in the
east joining the Allies in the west to hasten the final victory?*

ANSWER: *There need be no doubt that the Red Army will
fulfill its task with honor as it has been fulfilling it throughout the war.*

November 13, 1942

Dear Mr. Parker:

On May 3, I received your two questions concerning the Polish-Soviet relations. Here are my answers:

1. Does the Government of the U.S.S.R. desire to see a strong and independent Poland after the defeat of Hitler's Germany?

ANSWER: *Unquestionably, it does.*

2. On what fundaments is it your opinion the relations between Poland and the U.S.S.R. should be based after the war?

ANSWER: *Upon the fundament of solid good neighborly relations and mutual respect or, should the Polish people so desire, upon the fundament of an alliance providing for mutual assistance against the Germans as the chief enemies of the Soviet Union and Poland.*

May 4, 1943

4. REPLY TO LETTER FROM HAROLD KING, MOSCOW CORRESPONDENT OF REUTERS NEWS AGENCY

Dear Mr. King:

I have received your request to answer a question referring to the dissolution of the Communist International. I am sending you my answer.

QUESTION: *British comment on the decision to wind up the Comintern has been very favorable. What is the Soviet view of this matter and of its bearing on future international relations?*

ANSWER: *The dissolution of the Communist International is proper and timely because it facilitates the organization of* the common onslaught of all freedom-loving nations against the common enemy—Hitlerism. The dissolution of the Communist International is proper because:

1. It exposes the lie of the Hitlerites to the effect that Moscow allegedly intends to intervene in the life of other nations and to Bolshevize them. An end is now being put to this lie.

2. It exposes the calumny of adversaries of communism within the labor movement to the effect that Communist parties in various countries are allegedly acting not in the interest of their people but on orders from the outside. An end is now being put to this calumny, too.

3. It facilitates the work of patriots in freedom-loving countries for uniting progressive forces of their respective countries regardless of party or religious faith into a single camp of national liberation—for unfolding the struggle against fascism.

4. It facilitates the work of patriots in all countries for uniting all freedom-loving peoples into a single international camp for the fight against the menace of world domination by Hitlerism, thus clearing the way for future organization of a companionship based on their equality.

I think that all of these circumstances taken together will result in further strengthening of the united front of the Allies and other United Nations in the fight for victory over Hitlerite tyranny.

I feel that dissolution of the Communist International is perfectly timely because it is exactly now when the fascist beast is exerting its last strength that it is necessary to organize the common onslaught of freedom-loving countries to finish off this beast and deliver the peoples from fascist oppression.

May 28, 1943